BARNABAS MAM
with Kitti Murray

CHURCH
BEHIND THE
WIRE

A Story of FAITH
in the Killing Fields

MOODY PUBLISHERS
CHICAGO

© 2012 by
AMBASSADORS FOR CHRIST INTERNATIONAL

All Scripture quotations, unless otherwise indicated, are taken from *The Holy Bible, English Standard Version.* Copyright © 2000, 2001 by Crossway Bibles, a division of Good News Publishers. Used by permission. All rights reserved

Scripture quotations marked NIV are from the *Holy Bible: New International Version®.* NIV®. Copyright ©1973, 1978, 1984 by Biblica, Inc. Used by permission of Zondervan. All rights reserved worldwide.

Scripture quotations marked GNT are from the *Good News Translation*—Second Edition. Copyright ©1992 by American Bible Society. Used by permission.

Scripture quotations marked THE MESSAGE are from *The Message,* copyright © by Eugene H. Peterson 1993, 1994, 1995, 2000, 2001, 2002. Used by permission of NavPress Publishing Group.

Scripture quotations marked NLT are taken from the *Holy Bible, New Living Translation,* copyright © 1996, 2004, 2007. Used by permission of Tyndale House Publishers, Inc., Wheaton, Illinois 60189, U.S.A. All rights reserved.

Edited by Andy Scheer
Interior design: Ragont Design
Cover design: DBA Lucas Art & Design
Cover images: Masterfile and SuperStock

Library of Congress Cataloging-in-Publication Data

Mam, Barnabas, 1950-
  Church behind the wire : a story of faith in the killing fields / Barnabas Mam with Kitti Murray.
    p. cm.
  Includes bibliographical references and index.
  ISBN 978-0-8024-0597-5 (alk. paper)
    1. Mam, Barnabas, 1950- 2. Christian converts—Cambodia— Biography. 3. Conversion—Christianity—Biography. I. Murray, Kitti. II. Title.
BV4935.M26A3 2012
275.96'0825092--dc23
[B]

                                                      2012000542

We hope you enjoy this book from Moody Publishers. Our goal is to provide high-quality, thought-provoking books and products that connect truth to your real needs and challenges. For more information on other books and products written and produced from a biblical perspective, go to www.moodypublishers.com or write to:

Moody Publishers
820 N. LaSalle Boulevard
Chicago, IL 60610

1 3 5 7 9 10 8 6 4 2

Printed in the United States of America

CONTENTS

INTRODUCTION

For his anger is but for a moment,
and his favor is for a lifetime.
Weeping may tarry for the night,
but joy comes with the morning.

—Psalm 30:5

A **MOMENT** may last longer and the night may be darker for some than for others. When you weep, the world stands still. And the dawn takes its own sweet time. But in Christ, a lifetime means forever. Measure the night against a lifetime and there is no comparison. Place a moment in the context of a lifetime and it all but disappears.

My life has been punctuated with dark moments. Darker than most. Oh yes, I've lived in long seasons of night. Longer than most. But there has always been the dawn. And if you were to ask me today or tomorrow or even in the middle of that darkness, "Barnabas, how would you describe the flavor of your lifetime?" I would answer that my life has been defined by God's favor.

"How can you say such a thing?" you might ask. "You survived the Killing Fields in Cambodia. You witnessed the death of nearly one-fourth of the population of your homeland. You were often separated from your wife and children. You lived for eight years in the virtual prison of a refugee camp. You have known sickness, pain, and suffering that most of us in the West cannot fathom. Favor? Are you sure?"

I am sure. In another psalm David says, "In your light do we see light" (Psalm 36:9). To know God is to know things as they *really* are, in the light. So while my story is one of tragedy and loss, it is—overall—one of God's favor. I want to tell it honestly. I want you to know what it was like to live under the Khmer Rouge in the 1970s and

'80s. I want you to understand what happened—and then to see the ongoing effects of those years on my country. There is no doubt we have suffered—and still do. You'll see that.

But I also want you to join me in seeing things as they really were, to see the light in all that darkness. To see that God's favor directed me every step of the way: from the Buddhism of my childhood to the naïve Communism of my youth to finding Christ at a time when that discovery placed my life in danger. From finding food when there was none to answering my interrogators when I was arrested. From planting a church underground in Phnom Penh and later fifteen churches in the refugee camps in Thailand to galvanizing those churches for the eventual return to a Cambodia we could barely recognize.

I have seen God demonstrate His favor to the sick, the wounded, the suicidal, the hungry, the defeated. I want you to see Him too. To taste the way He has flavored my life. His favor—defined by Scripture not circumstances but in the context of a relationship with Him—is the reason this story is ultimately one of hope and healing. That's what I want you to see. That's the joy that comes in the morning.

TIME LINE

900–1500 AD	Khmer Empire
1863–1953	Cambodia is a French protectorate.
1950	***Birth of Barnabas Mam***
1953	Cambodia peacefully gains independence from France under Prince Sihanouk.
1970	Lon Nol leads coup against Prince Sihanouk.
1972	***Barnabas becomes a believer in Jesus Christ at World Vision Crusade.***
1972–1975	***Barnabas works for World Vision offices in Phnom Penh.***
1970–1975	Cambodian civil war
April 17, 1975	Siege of Phnom Penh by Pol Pot. Other major cities soon fall.
1975–1979	The Killing Fields exist throughout Cambodia under Pol Pot and the Khmer Rouge.

	Barnabas spends the majority of these years in several hastily constructed prison camps. He lives over half of this time in two camps: Sambok Moan and Svay Don Keo.
1979	Vietnamese occupation of Cambodia begins.
	Barnabas returns to Phnom Penh, marries Boury, their daughter Shalom is born, and Barnabas becomes a worship leader in the underground church.
1985	*Boury and Barnabas, with three of their children, begin their eleven-month flight to Thailand.*
1985–1993	*The Mam family lives in Site II refugee camp in Thailand.*
1989	Vietnam withdraws from Cambodia. UN peace talks fail to reach agreement.
1991	Paris Peace Accord guarantees freedom in Cambodia's constitution. UN mission to Cambodia begins.
1992	Congress of Cambodian Communist Party resolves to permit religious freedom to Buddhists, Muslims, and Christians. Christians can meet in public for the first time since 1975.
1993	*Barnabas and family return to Cambodia.*
1998	Pol Pot dies.

Chapter One

ON THE HEELS
OF CIVIL WAR

The Killing Fields

No places to hide,
no skies under which to rest;
and the moaning of children
and the cries of mothers
out of blazing fire across the land.[1]

—From *Only Mothers Will Embrace Sorrows* by U Sam Oeur,
poet and army captain in the American-backed
Cambodian government of Gen. Lon Nol

All wars are civil wars,
because all men are brothers.

—Francois Fenelon

IT'S A common question in college ethics classes: If you were hungry enough, would you feel justified in stealing a loaf of bread? Perhaps you've engaged in a lively theoretical discussion about this. But it's difficult to have an honest debate when your stomach has never really known hunger, when you have never been desperate enough to consider theft as your only means of survival.

My sister Boran did not live long enough to debate with anyone on the subject. Like me, she was born in Cambodia at a time when hunger was anything but theoretical. But Boran was never imprisoned like I was, unless you consider that our entire nation was locked in the prison-state of Pol Pot's extreme Communist ideology and his murderous web of leadership.

You may have heard of the Killing Fields. You may even know it is a five-year epoch that fits somewhere in the complex history of the Vietnam War. Although there are specific places in the Cambodian countryside where the bones of our people still emerge from the ground after a heavy rain, the phrase aptly describes our entire nation from 1975 until 1979.

Early in those years Boran was assigned work in a communal garden in her village. All Cambodians were given subsistence jobs in what Pol Pot called "the great leap forward." But the harder we worked, the less we moved forward. By the time the harvest came in Boran's village, she was weak and hungry enough to steal. She kept back a few of the scrawniest sweet potatoes for herself.

The field was guarded by young boys called *chhlops*, or spies. One saw Boran slip a potato in her pocket and alerted a *cadre*. This thirteen-year-old officer beat her to death with her own shovel—not even bothering to remove the sweet potatoes from her pocket.

I did not hear of Boran's death until several years later. She died alone, isolated by the madness of a genocidal, paranoid regime, and was hastily buried. Between 1975 and 1979, nearly one-fourth of our population died. Like my own father and a host of my friends, many starved to death or died of disease. Even more were executed for crimes as slight as continuing to wear eyeglasses—which signified elitism in the minds of our leaders—or stealing barely enough food to live for one more day.

Beginning with the time of the Killing Fields and ending in 1989 when Vietnam withdrew from Cambodia, I was guilty of a crime—one that was ultimately punishable by death. I was a follower of Christ. Not only that, I was a leader in the church, both before Pol Pot and the Khmer Rouge deemed all religions subversive and after the nationwide paralysis of the Killing Fields when the church, to survive, grew underground.

As you'll read, there were many times when the only thing that separated me from a martyr's fate was a miracle. Miracles that, in light of a mounting tally of Christian martyrdom, were hard to understand.

When I heard about Boran, I wondered why God allowed me to live. Now, that's a question for the ethics classes. Why did I survive when so many I loved did not? I don't have a tidy answer. But I am sure of one reason: so I could tell you my story.

The Nightmare Emerges

I remember the first time I heard the term *the Killing Fields.*

I'm not sure when the rest of the world heard it. Perhaps it was not long after 1979 when Ho Van Tay, a Vietnamese combat photographer, followed the stench of rotting human remains to the gates of Tuol Sleng[2] prison and documented his discovery to the world. In a moment reminiscent of the liberation of Dachau in Germany or Auschwitz-Birkenau in Poland at the end of World War II, I can only imagine Tay's horror as the truth assaulted his senses and he realized what he'd stumbled upon.

If you are *there* for a genocide,
it is your nightmare.
Your memory.
Something you can never forget.

I'm not sure when the Western world became aware that the Killing Fields had been the grim reality of our nation. Or when memorials began to rise upon the very ground where tourists felt the crunch of human bones beneath their feet and peered at photographs of prisoners—men, boys, pregnant women, babies, girls—some posing as if sitting for a solemn portrait and others with the frightened eyes of the doomed.

I am not sure when the records of those prisoners emerged with their short biographies that began with their occupations, mostly farmers, and ended with a cryptic "smashed"[3] to indicate the efficient way the Khmer Rouge disposed of its enemies—its own people—and in the process spared their bullets for the Viet Cong. I don't know when our own tragedy became known to the world, only to be forgotten when the next genocide hit the newsstands.

That's what genocide is—something everyone would rather forget. Something so irredeemable we cannot consider it too long for fear the grief of its existence anywhere in the world will swallow us whole. A nightmare.

But if you are *there* for a genocide, it is your nightmare. Your memory. Something you can never forget.

When I first heard the words *the Killing Fields*, I was close enough for the woman who said them to point and add, "Over there." I was 26 years old. It was the end of 1978 and the killing of my own people by the Khmer Rouge, also my own people, had escalated until at least one in five of our population lay dead.[4] Our stories are alike in that they are solitary and they are senseless. And none of us saw it coming.

Idealism and What I Did with Mine

A civil war was brewing in my homeland when I came of age in the late 1960s and early 1970s. Like many young men who grow up during a time of dramatic polarities, I was an idealist. And because I was young, I was also impressionable.

At first the two lines behind which men fought for power in Cambodia were not drawn very boldly. Some were loyal to our exiled Prince Sihanouk and, by default, to the burgeoning Communist Party. What eventually became the Khmer Rouge began as a collection of groups —some more like cults—that embraced varying Communist ideologies. Eventually under Pol Pot, most of these groups melded into one.

Then there were those who supported Lon Nol, the American-backed general who had overthrown Sihanouk in 1970. Sihanouk had peacefully negotiated our independence from France in 1953, and he was widely considered a brilliant diplomat. Under his rule, Cambodia remained neutral while war raged in our neighboring countries. But many felt he was too sympathetic to the North Vietnamese, which rendered him dangerous to the United States and vulnerable to a coup by his own general, Lon Nol.

Most of my family was loyal to the reigning regime, to Lon Nol's Republicans who were fighting the Communists. By the time I was 20, I had joined the Maquis, one of the more benign—so I thought—Communist factions. But I was naïve. I thought the nationalist sentiments embraced by the Maquis would steer our country in the right direction. I was disenchanted with the French colonialism of our past and with the American-backed government of Lon Nol. I supported the return of Prince Sihanouk, in exile in Beijing, who had responded to Lon Nol's coup by aligning himself with Mao Zedong's Cultural Revolution. Wanting to bring about change, I joined the Maquis, or, as it is translated from the French, "The Jungle."

Genocide often begins with the pretext of "the greater good" and ends with any horrific means to achieve it. To perpetrate the myth, the reigning power uses children, teenagers, or very young adults. I wonder if those pliable young men who looted Jewish businesses for the Nazi regime on the infamous Kristallnacht in Germany—"the night of broken glass"—began like I did. Were they enamored with a noble idea? Did they really believe the propaganda that hoodwinked so many?

I see pictures of skinny boy soldiers shouldering AK-47s in Rwanda or Sierra Leone and cannot imagine how an idea can germinate in a young mind and grow to such dreadful proportions. Are these young boys victims, criminals, or simply mistaken? Did they pick up a rock, a stick, or an automatic weapon because, somehow, that made sense in the grand scheme of their leader's politics?

Later, during the years of the Killing Fields in Cambodia, young boys were used as *chhlops*, spies. By the time a boy reached 13, he was promoted. He became a soldier.

I was not a Communist long enough to be forced to become a soldier. Even so, most who remained loyal to the ideals I embraced while I was in the Maquis watched in horror as our ideals were twisted into a rationale for mass murder.

My Communist mentor told me any sacrifice I made would contribute to the greater good: to loving, rebuilding, and protecting Cambodia.

I joined this particular group of Communist activists because I was a patriot who believed in peace. I don't know if, had I remained in the Maquis, I would have succumbed to the "kill or be killed" pressure that trapped many of the *cadres* (officers) in the makeshift prisons that pocked the Cambodian countryside. The killings occurred in growing numbers from 1975, when Pol Pot and the Democratic Kampuchea (Kampuchea is the original name for Cambodia) seized Phnom Penh from Lon Nol, until 1979, when the Vietnamese army invaded and forced him to retreat.

Toward the end, a frenzy of paranoia reigned, and it really didn't matter where your loyalties lay. You could be executed—either swiftly with a blow to the back of the head with a hoe or a metal pipe or slowly by daily beatings and torture—for offenses as insignificant as using a foreign word, showing affection to your wife, or even having more than one syllable in your name. Idealism had become insanity.

While the civil war festered, before it became the open wound of the Killing Fields, my idealism never led me to do the unthinkable, to take human life. But because of that idealism, I did some pretty inane things. The Communists taught us to relinquish all things personal in favor of the communal. I believed that I as an individual was insignificant in light of the collective society.

My Communist mentor, Mr. At Veth, who was my yoga instructor and literature teacher, told me any sacrifice I made would contribute to the greater good: to loving, rebuilding, and protecting Cambodia. And so, because of an ideal, I chopped a syllable off my name. My parents named me Sovann, which means gold; I changed it to Vann.

You may think the meaning of my name was the reason I felt I had to change it. The wealthy were, as they were to all Communist sects in Asia, suspect. Ownership—of anything—was considered a liability. Eventually gold itself became worthless. And those who possessed it were held in savage contempt.

But it wasn't what my name implied that led me to change it; it was how it *sounded*. Changing my name represented a small leap from an idea to an action. Back then, it made perfect sense. In the new Cambodia no one should have more syllables in their name than anyone else. To leave the old life behind and create a new unified world order, wouldn't it be simpler to all have one-syllable names?

So I did to my name what the Khmer Rouge eventually did to all of us: I diminished it. My name, like everything and everyone around me, became so small, it almost disappeared. My new name symbolized what would happen to Phnom Penh's population in the next few years: it would be cut in half.

I was a small young man, barely an adult, with a small name and, I soon realized, a small vision. What I failed to see was that the Khmer Rouge would soon drive all of Cambodia out of our cities and into the jungle. The Maquis would become our home for almost five years.

The Safe and the Unsafe

On April 17, 1975, Pol Pot seized Phnom Penh. I along with one million others fled the city. The civil war was over and the revolution had won. The pretense for this evacuation, repeated over and over on loudspeakers mounted on Khmer Rouge Jeeps that swarmed through the city, was that American bombers were on the way, and we all believed it. But the bombers never came, and the bombs never fell.

If the Americans were doing anything, it was exactly what we were doing: leaving. Under Lon Nol, foreign soldiers, diplomats, and journalists had been welcome, or at least tolerated, in Phnom Penh. The night before the siege, the Westerners living in the capital received word that the invasion would happen the next day.

While we were shuffled out of the city to shouted commands underscored with automatic weapon fire, helicopters landed at the US Embassy. Two hundred and seventy-six people left the country on CH-53 helicopters that had flown to Cambodia from two American aircraft carriers. Although several Khmer rockets landed on neighboring buildings, "Operation Eagle Pull" was considered a flawless rescue.[5]

The civil war was indeed over. But the killing wasn't, not by a long shot. Four days later, on April 21, 1975, *Time* magazine reported, in a bizarre ironic twist, "Although there is no such thing as a graceful ending to five years of fratricidal bloodshed, it may still be possible to make the inevitable transfer of power in Phnom Penh without subjecting its civilians to the ultimate tragedy of an all-out military assault."[6]

Meanwhile, we citizens of Phnom Penh made a bewildered exit on foot as quickly as we could. Pol Pot considered April 17 day one of his "Year Zero," a literal voiding of Cambodia, a total deconstruction the Khmer Rouge felt was necessary to reconstruct the nation into an agrarian, Communist society.

All we were told was that we would be gone for three days, but half of us never returned. The other half spent the next four years in the jungle, either in one of many hastily constructed prisons or subsisting as forced laborers in the rice fields. We were driven into the countryside and stripped of everything we owned: currency, education, property. The lost syllables of our names were nothing compared to the other losses: our culture, our identity, our homes, our ancient religions.

Soon I and thousands of my countrymen living with me in the jungle realized we were trapped. There were no choppers on the way to save us. We were alone. All but forgotten. Along with starvation and slaughter, suicides became commonplace. We were caught in a desperate place with no hope for rescue. As one of us later wrote, "Now that the revolution had come, we had been bulldozed by it, reduced to the same level as the other exiles around us. And there was no society building. Just the rubble of the old one."[7]

With the sudden ferocity of a thunderstorm, fratricide turned into genocide.

Notes

1. U Sam Oeur, *Sacred Vows* (Minneapolis: Coffee House Press, 1998), 35.

2. Tuol Sleng was a high school that the Khmer Rouge converted into a prison. It was notorious for torture of political prisoners. The commandant, Duch, faced the International Court in Cambodia in 2007.

3. The term "smashed" was used repeatedly—in parentheses next to a name—to describe executions in the prison records at Tuol Sleng.

4. Estimates range from 1.7 to 2 million dead during the Killing Fields.

5. "Cambodia: American Pullout from a City Under Siege," *Time*, April 21, 1975. www.time.com/time/magazine/article/0,9171,917322-1,00.html#ixzz11QeAlq8N.

6. Ibid.

7. Haing Ngor with Roger Warner. *Survival in the Killing Fields* (New York: Carroll & Graf, 1987), 119.

Chapter Two

WHAT HOPE
SOUNDS LIKE

Worshiping in Hell

He put a new song in my mouth,
a song of praise to our God.
Many will see and fear,
and put their trust in the Lord.

—Psalm 40:3

Communism is not love.

—Mao Zedong

DURING THE Killing Fields, survival was a miracle. Suffering was a given. But there is much more to my story. To tell it properly, I have to go back to 1972, three years before the siege of Phnom Penh, to the day I left Communism.

When I left the Maquis, everyone knew it. I did not formally resign. I did not write a letter or show up at a meeting to give a farewell speech. But I did leave. As completely as we exited Phnom Penh a few years later, I left the Communist movement.

My comrades in the Maquis and I knew something that made staying impossible: No one can serve two masters. And I had bowed my knee to a new master, to Jesus Christ. As I will explain in detail later, I responded to the gospel on the very first evening I heard it. Afterward my mentor, Mr. At Veth, sent messengers to convince me I'd made a terrible mistake. They promised I could return honorably. At that time there was still honor in Cambodia. We still respected each other, and our differences had not yet driven us to the wholesale slaughter that followed the civil war.

Finally, At Veth sent me a message: "I release you." He understood I was never coming back. Instead of trusting in an idea to change our country, I now knew a Savior who could change *me*.

The human heart has always needed a Rescuer, a Deliverer. Someone to change what *is* to what *can be*. From Adam and Eve's first steps out of the garden—the only perfect government mankind has ever known—we have longed to be liberated from the imperfect world in which we live.

As a nation we craved hope so badly, we were willing to enter a civil war to find it.

Every one of us lives in a Maquis, a jungle. And we all, every one of us, long for a garden. Yes, there are seasons when it seems as if we live in a garden. Life is good. We have plenty of food and water, family, and friendship. We are thriving and happy. But more often we can't help but know we live in a broken, troubled world—a jungle. This is true on every scale: in our personal lives and in our communities. And it is true globally. We have witnessed the utter brokenness of the human race many times in the past century: in Nazi Germany, in Uganda, in Albania, in Bosnia, and in Darfur. Cambodia's experience echoes these tragedies. One cannot survive the genocide of one's own people and not know something is terribly wrong with all of humanity.

But even in the best of times, our need for deliverance is an ever-present fact of life. That's why we're always searching for ways to make life better. That's why I left the Buddhism of my youth to join a group of Communist activists. Even before things went from bad to worse, I had instinctively known that things *could* be better. I had a hint that the Deliverer existed; I just didn't know Him yet. So I looked for deliverance in the only place I thought I might find it: in the Communist ideal.

I found the only true Deliverer, Jesus, before the Khmer Rouge came to full power. Until then, like my Communist mentor, I placed my hope for a better Cambodia, a better *life*, in an ideology. Like my mentor, I counted the cost and aligned myself with the revolution. Although my parents and most of my siblings were on opposite poles from me politically, we all craved the same thing. We did not yet realize we needed a Deliverer, but we all longed for the hope of one. As a nation we craved hope so badly, we were willing to enter a civil war to find it. I loved my family, but I was passionate enough to defy them in my pursuit of hope.

What I didn't know yet is that no political liberator, no cultural messiah, no social savior can rescue us from the jungle we all live in. No human ideology, however noble and pure, can counteract the effects of that jungle. No government system can make things right.

I am grateful I learned these truths before the siege of Phnom Penh, before my arrest, before the physical suffering of those years, before the Killing Fields, before my family's exile to Thailand. Otherwise my life might have ended like my mentor's. He died in Tuol Sleng prison. Like many others, he killed himself before the *cadres* had a chance to.

My mentor was like all of us. He lived in a jungle, and he longed for a garden. He was naïve enough to believe a political movement could rescue our country from brokenness and bring wholeness. He not only needed a Deliverer, he also needed the hope of one. When I knew him, he was a hopeful man. But that hope was misplaced, so it did not serve him in the end. The tragedy of his life runs deeper than his death in Tuol Sleng. He died without something we all need so badly: hope.

What Hope Sounds Like

When we fled Phnom Penh in 1975, I had been a follower of Jesus for only three years. Considering the facts of my life for the next years, you might wonder that I call God my Deliverer. What kind of Deliverer was He? Did He deliver me from sickness, danger, hunger, or loss? No, these were my constant companions. From imprisonment, hardship, or sorrow? No, I experienced these in full measure.

It is human nature to think we must have deliverance *from* something, when usually our souls truly need deliverance *in* that something. This is the essence of hope. And this is the sound I began to hear. Hope is a portable gift, given by God and carried with the believer into any circumstance. Hope defies hopeless situations. In fact, hope often stands in complete opposition to the reality we see around us.

When we left Phnom Penh, most people were driven on foot out of the city into the country. I left in the company of friends, but soon I was traveling alone with masses of strangers. Near the Vietnam border, I was arrested and sent to a "reeducation camp." I spent more than a year imprisoned in a camp called Sambok Moan. One year, three months, and thirteen days.

It's funny how in the midst of monumental suffering, the small things can hurt the most. In one of the most ancient accounts in the Old Testament, we see how a man named Job lost his home, his wealth, and his children. He suffered on every possible front, but the boils that erupted all over his body were almost his undoing.

Ringworms were my last straw. During my imprisonment at Sambok Moan, my face was covered with them. They itched terribly, especially when it rained. Not only were they a source of constant discomfort, I also wondered if the scars that were sure to remain for the rest of my life would make me repulsive. Who would love or associate with a man who looked like me? I tried every possible remedy, including eating chicken with black legs and rubbing my face with the tarlike sap of a certain tree, all to no avail.

The population of the prison rose and fell, eventually dwindling from more than 300 to 127. Every day we battled the pain of hunger and illness. I had friends who were imprisoned with me, and they began to die one by one. I was the only one who volunteered to bury them. I wrapped each body in a palm leaf mat, tied both ends, and carried it to any available spot. Each time, I wondered who would do the honors for me when I died.

As I stood, itching and in pain,
grieving the loss of my home
and my family and friends,
I had a vision of the church worldwide, worshiping along with me.

Eventually, I ran out of space for these burials, so I began to cremate the bodies of my friends. I did not have a lighter or a flint, so each time I cut a section of bamboo shoot and placed a dry piece of cotton from a *kapok* tree inside it. Then, with a shard of pottery and a broken knife blade, I ignited the *kapok*. During one makeshift cremation, it began to rain. The fire charred my friend's body and turned it black. Then the fire died. The rain washed open a nearby shallow grave, so I decided to bury him there. In the process, the oily, smelly water of the grave splashed on my face. I cried out to God to help me bear it, as I finished burying yet another friend.

During one particularly violent thunderstorm, I stood at a window and sang hymns, the only Christian songs I knew. These rainstorms were a gift because I could sing without being heard. I sang "How Great Thou Art" out loud in Khmer, French, and English. I was not a professional singer, but I had a song in my heart. And that song gave me a very substantial hope. As I stood, itching and in pain, shaking with the fever of malaria, grieving the loss of my home and my family and friends, I had a vision of the church worldwide, worshiping along with me. I was not alone. And I was—miraculously—at peace.

Another song I learned as a new believer was the hymn "When the Roll Is Called up Yonder." When it rained at Sambok Moan and I sang that hymn out loud, I often believed the heavenly roll call was going to utter my name at any moment. The *Angkar* (or "organization," the common name for the Khmer Rouge government) threatened to send me "up yonder" every day.

Each morning and evening in prison, we were counted by roll call so our captors would know how many of us had just died. I longed for that "bright and cloudless morning when the dead in Christ shall rise, and the glory of His resurrection share." The Communists had a saying: "To take him away (to kill him) is no loss. To keep him with us is no gain." I preferred Paul's sentiment: "For me to live is Christ, and to die is gain" (Philippians 1:21).

When I compared my earthly existence to the one I anticipated in heaven, I was more than ready to leave the ugliness of earth for the beauty of heaven. But because I knew God and had the privilege to worship Him, to "talk of all His wondrous love and care," I was thankful for every day I answered that prison roll call, for every day I was still alive.

I loved the old hymns because they helped me concentrate on God Himself instead of on my surroundings. But I really learned to trust and worship Him when I read the ancient songs of an even earlier time. Day after day and night after night, I meditated on David's Psalm 23:

> The Lord is my shepherd; I shall not want. He makes me lie down in green pastures. He leads me beside still waters. He restores my soul. He leads me in paths of righteousness for his name's sake. Even though I walk through the valley of the shadow of death, I will fear no evil, for you are with me; your rod and your staff, they comfort me. You prepare a table before me in the presence of my enemies; you anoint my head with oil; my cup overflows. Surely goodness and mercy shall follow me all the days of my life, and I shall dwell in the house of the Lord forever.

Over time, every phrase of this psalm came alive. I began to see that the Lord is, indeed, my Shepherd, and if I will let Him lead me, I *shall not* want.

I Shall Not Want

Even before the long months in Sambok Moan, I saw evidence of the realities described in Psalm 23. I saw God provide on that bewildering day in 1975 when the Khmer Rouge seized Phnom Penh. The mass exodus was swift and absolute. Because we were led to believe it was temporary, no one packed more than they could carry. Those who were rich brought items that quickly became obsolete, like gold and currency. The poor fared better because they carried food and cooking utensils, and they knew how to live off of the land.

I was praying at the World Vision child care office on April 17, 1975, the day of the evacuation. The Khmer Rouge marched through the streets chanting victory songs. A loudspeaker broadcast the government radio station: "April 17, 1975, is a day of great victory of tremendous historical significance for our Cambodian nation and people! . . . Long live the independent, peaceful, neutral, nonaligned, sovereign, democratic and prosperous Cambodia with genuine territorial integrity!"[1]

I left the office with my friend Song. We went first to my home to search for my family but found our house empty. We then went to Song's home and discovered his family had left just hours before. Back in the streets, we were told to head east. I left Phnom Penh with only the clothes on my back and my *kramar* (a traditional Cambodian all-purpose scarf).

On my way out of the city, Song and I met some Christian friends, including Timothy and his fiancée, her mother, and her siblings. Next, we met some teenagers who attended the Sunday school class I taught. The teens were separated from their families, so they joined us. A few widows from our church saw us, and we invited them to walk with us as well. Soon there were eighteen of us traveling on foot together. Almost immediately, I became the leader of our group because I, though younger than some of them, was the oldest in the faith. Just as immediately, I inherited the responsibility of finding food for all eighteen of us.

Hunger. Want. It had already begun. It was a predicament shared by all one million people who left Phnom Penh that day. Later, when thousands were dying daily from malnourishment and starvation, the solution was not so simple. But on this day food was a mere swim across a river or a walk across a bridge away. It was right there, in plain sight. There was plenty of it in the restaurants and warehouses and homes of Phnom Penh, but we were forbidden to return. And that prohibition was emphasized by the bloated bodies floating in each of the four rivers that mark the periphery of Phnom Penh. Later, the Khmer Rouge would kill more inventively, preferring not to squander their bullets. But on this day anyone caught returning to the city was shot.

But the little ones in our group of eighteen were whimpering for food. We prayed together, then Timothy and I turned back. Many people risked their lives that day by crossing the rivers on bamboo rafts. We felt the Holy Spirit's prompting to walk back along Route Number One, across the Monivong Bridge that spans the Bassac River, into the city. We strode in full view of a group of combatants. One, who guarded the entrance to the city from his Jeep, was an old classmate. I almost greeted him, but I sensed the Holy Spirit directing me, and I pretended not to know him. I could tell he recognized me, but he didn't make eye contact. To have a friend from the city would have endangered his life.

Timothy and I walked to the closest warehouse where we found plenty of rice. Hundreds of large bags were stacked to the ceiling, and a mob frantically pulled bags from the bottom of the stacks. My human instinct was to join the panic and pull a few bags myself, but I stopped and held an arm across Timothy's chest to stop him. It seemed the Spirit told me to hang back, so we did. We barely had time to enter the warehouse and observe the scene when the stacks collapsed, crushing some of the men.[2] As the bags of rice fell, one flew through the air and landed at my feet. It was stenciled with the words *Donated by the US Government,* but in my heart I thanked the true Giver of this gift. I found a bicycle and placed the bag on it. Timothy and I then wheeled our rice out of the city and crossed the same bridge, again in full sight of my friend and his companions.

So began a long journey of learning to trust in my ultimate Deliverer, to rely on the nudges of the Holy Spirit, and to proclaim, even when the hunger pangs gnawed at my stomach, "I shall not want." This knowledge is the seedbed of true worship. When all else is stripped away, God is still God. Most of the estimated two hundred followers of Christ who survived the Killing Fields did so without any contact with other Christians to encourage us. But the prevailing fact of God's goodness did not change.

Perhaps it does not make sense to begin a story about suffering with a song, but that is how this one begins. The real miracle in my story is that God is faithful, that He proves His faithfulness even in the direst of circumstances, and that He is to be worshiped.

For me, that is the miracle of the Killing Fields: God drew me inexorably toward Himself, and I worshiped.

Notes

1. Haing Ngor, *Survival in the Killing Fields* (New York: Carroll & Graf, 1987), 98.

2. This story is corroborated in Ngor's book, page 102.

Chapter Three

I SPY

With Unexpected Results

" 'Well, I'll soon have that out of you. I have none o'yer bawling, praying, singing . . . on my place; so remember. Now mind yourself' he said with a stamp and a fierce glance of his gray eye, directed at Tom, 'I'm your church now! You understand,—you've got to be as I say.' "[1]

—Simon Legree in *Uncle Tom's Cabin*

No one saves us but ourselves.
No one can and no one may.
We ourselves must walk the path.

—Buddha

Salvation belongs to the Lord.

—Psalm 3:8

AS A young man, if I believed in anything, it was in the certainty of nothingness. As a Buddhist, I had been taught the doctrine of *anatman*, or nonsoul. Then I became a Communist who believed, not necessarily that the soul does not exist but that it doesn't matter because "the people" matter more. As a Buddhist, I had rejected the idea that there was any real beginning or ending to the earth. As a Communist and a Darwinist, beginnings and endings belonged to science. So how we got here in the beginning and where we went in the end did not matter.

What mattered most to me was my nation. During my late teens and early twenties, if I stood *for* anything, it was Cambodia. My country had been stripped of its unique ethnicity during the French colonial period. Our prince—our political redeemer, the one who freed us from French rule—lived in exile. His enemies, the Republican government of Lon Nol, had wrested the country from Prince Sihanouk and, in our view, given it to the Americans. So everything with an American label was our enemy. That included Christians.

Herein lies the allure of political movements. The soul—which I now know does indeed exist—was created to care about *something*. That's why so many of my friends and I were ripe for the radical claims of Marxism. We were tired of Buddhism's complacency. We were young and full of life. The revolution challenged our minds. It was, well, revolutionary. Besides, we had an intense need to commit to something that mattered.

Our country needed us, so we took sides. We found a knight in shining armor to follow and, by default, an enemy to defeat. I was caught up in a noble cause that I believed in with all my heart. It was my "good news." So what good was the gospel to someone like me? I belonged to a tight-knit community of friends, intellectuals, students, and teachers. I had a mentor who loved me. I did not know—or even care—who Jesus Christ was. I had no idea what Christians believed. In many ways I was a blank slate.

I was an evangelist's dream. Or his worst nightmare.

What Good Was the Gospel?

To be honest, my slate wasn't completely blank. In my childhood I'd had one memorable encounter with the Bible. And I profited from it, in a way.

I was born into a large family. My father's first wife died and left him with two sons. My mother's first husband died and left her with three daughters. After my mother and father married, they had four more children together, two daughters and two sons. Of the nine children in our blended family, I was the seventh.

I was a small, scrappy child. Like most smaller children, I found ways to compensate for my size on the playground. But sometimes my small stature caused problems. Riding a bicycle was more difficult for me than it was for my peers. That posed a problem later, when I attended high school twenty kilometers away from our village.

I loved my older half sisters, especially Sovannary, who was a teacher. Every year or so, she transferred to a school in a new location, and when she did, she took me with her. Through her, I learned to love reading and learning. And through my travels with Sovannary, I also learned to love Cambodia and the Khmer people.

When I was little, the most valuable currency for young village children was rubber bands. We traded or gambled to get them. The more a boy had, the richer he was. I coveted rubber bands but could never collect as many as I wanted. Until Sovannary gave me the book.

It was a children's storybook filled with colorful illustrations of men with long hair and beards, wearing flowing robes. I'm not sure where she got it, but my sister explained that this book contained Bible stories about a man named Jesus. I became obsessed with that book. I read it every day. I became familiar with the images, though I could not understand the words. I had a vague respect for this Jesus because in most of the pictures He seemed to be healing or helping people. To my young eyes, the lush vegetation of Palestine looked a lot like the rain forests of Cambodia. I valued the book because it interested me personally. But I also knew an opportunity when I saw one.

As often as I could, I whipped out my prized possession to show my friends. Soon the novelty wore off, so I created a game: "Close your eyes," I would say to a buddy, "and point to a page."

If the page my friend pointed to had fewer people on it than the opposite page, I won one of his rubber bands. If he chose the page with a greater number of people, I had to give him one of mine. The book was my lucky charm! I collected so many rubber bands, I wove them into a garland and wore it everywhere. The gospel, or a multicolored children's book that illustrated it, had made me rich.

Much later, as a young Communist, I again schemed to profit from the gospel. This time, though I still did not yet understand the message of Christ, the stakes were much higher.

Undercover

For me, Communism was a cultlike experience. My mentor, Mr. At Veth, was, above all, my friend. When I first began attending his classes, I did not know he was a Communist. He was kind and compassionate. He cared about the things I cared about, so I trusted him.

I trusted him when he asked me to write by hand a Khmer translation of *Uncle Tom's Cabin.* He said it was an exposé of American imperialism and the harm it had inflicted upon an entire race. I trusted him when he talked in glowing terms of the Cultural Revolution in China and the genius of Mao Zedong. I trusted him when he held up the Russian revolution as a paradigm worth emulating. And I trusted him when he finally revealed he was a member of the Maquis.

In a final act of trust I allowed him to do what he had planned all along, to enlist me into his group of Communist activists. And then, like At Veth, I began to recruit young students for the movement. I trusted him, and my mentor trusted me. That's why he sent me to spy on the enemy camp.

It was the spring of 1972. The Christians were in town, and they caused quite a stir. Dr. Stan Mooneyham, at that time the president of World Vision, conducted two evangelistic crusades in Phnom Penh that year. Both were held at the city's largest venue, the Chaktomuk Conference Hall. The hall wasn't large enough for the masses of people who mobbed the courtyard on the first night of the April crusade. It could hold only 1,200 people. On that first night 6,000 people were turned away. To ensure every person heard the gospel, Dr. Mooneyham preached twice on the second and third nights, once at a "pre-crusade" outside on the lawn to more than 2,000, then again inside to a capacity crowd.

This was a patently American event. At least that's what we Communists thought. Remember, the Maquis was an ideological movement. We had not read, or we chose not to remember, the darker side of Mao's message. Most of us, Mr. At Veth included, signed up to change our country, not to hurt it. I'm not sure we ever really considered the consequences of following the truly revolutionary claims Mao made, such as, "A revolution is an insurrection; an act of violence by which one class overthrows another,"[2] or "Communism is not love. Communism is a hammer which we use to crush the enemy."[3]

We were probably more committed than we cared to admit to our Buddhist heritage of nonviolence. Perhaps if we had paid closer attention to the prototype, China's Cultural Revolution, or listened more carefully to the words of its leader, we would have seen what lay ahead for us in Cambodia.

All I knew was that the Christians, because they were influenced by the Americans, were up to no good. So we needed to know just how bad things were. We needed to know who had joined the enemy. Therefore we needed to infiltrate.

Mr. At Veth asked me to attend the second night of the April crusade as a spy. I tried to arrive early, following the crowds who gathered on Sisowath Quay, the street that runs between the Mekong River and Chaktomuk Conference Hall.

It was easy to blend in. I joined hundreds of young people who swarmed into the building from the neatly manicured courtyard with its geometric grid of lawns divided by concrete sidewalks. The hall was designed by one of Cambodia's most famous architects, Vann Molyvann.

After recent renovations it remains today an imposing combination of a Khmer-style pagoda and glass and steel modernity.

That night, I wasn't the only spy skulking in the shadows. Just about every political faction of the civil war, most of them Communist, planted someone like me in that meeting. The fact that I knew they were there means none of us was all that covert. But espionage and its close cousin, paranoia, were already part of our culture. In the next few years the Khmer Rouge would catapult suspicion to new heights.

I wore the uniform of a student: dark blue pants and a white shirt. I carried a notebook and a book, thinking that would make me look like "one of them." I put on my glasses and sat in a row near the back corner of the fan-shaped auditorium so I could see everything—and if necessary make a quick exit. I scanned the crowd as I perched on the edge of my seat and waited for the main speaker to utter his first words, words I was sure would condemn him.

I Didn't Seek Him; He Sought Me.

What does it take to bring a Buddhist-turned-Communist to Christ? What reasoning will pry him from his belief in a man-centered universe in which God is only a human invention? What kind of brilliant expository preaching is required to explain the good news to someone who has never heard it?

That night I was by no means a "seeker." At least I didn't think I was. Buddhism had taught me the individual soul does not exist. Communism taught me it doesn't matter. My soul, if I had one, did not need saving. I was there to profit in one way only, to gather information that would indict the enemy. But I was to profit in a way that affirmed the very thing I rejected.

A group of African-American women called the Danniebelles sang several numbers at the beginning of the program. Danniebelle Hall and the other women sang with an enthusiasm that seemed genuine, but I tuned them out so I could watch the crowd.

Then Dr. Stanley Mooneyham stood up to speak. He stayed silent for a moment as he removed his wristwatch. I expected him to lay it on the lectern as a reminder to keep his talk the proper length, something only an American would do. But he held the watch up in his right hand, slowly waved it before us, then laid it down in one fluid, dramatic movement. He paused for a moment, then said, "If my watch was laid here on the lectern before you in a hundred pieces, does it seem plausible to you that a 'big bang' could occur—and in a split second my watch could assemble itself into perfect working order?"

"No!" thundered a thousand voices.

"Consider the traffic in Phnom Penh. Does it flow in perfect working order without one single accident?"

Again—this time mingled with a few chuckles—the collective cry, "No!"

"Now consider the stars and planets, thousands upon thousands, all aligned above us in perfect order. Night after night there are no accidents. No wrong turns or collisions. No mistakes. Could one bang have resulted in this kind of exquisite order?"

"No!"

"Who, then, created the lights we see in the night sky? Who made those we do not see? Who holds our planetary system—a system far more intricate than the traffic here in your beautiful city—in perfect order?"

In the silence I realized I was holding my breath, longing for the answer. I completely forgot my mission. I forgot to scrutinize the crowd, to locate the leaders near the front and write their names. I forgot everything but this question: Who created me? And could I, as Dr. Mooneyham asserted next in what seemed a U-turn in his logic, could I really know this alleged Creator?

For the first time in my life, the beginning—of the earth, of life, of *my* life—mattered to me. A split second of common sense was all it took to debunk my naïve Darwinism. I soon understood that a loving Creator God was behind all of the precision and beauty of life. This realization was remarkable enough, but Mooneyham had more to say.

What I heard next was a story. It was a story, he explained, that illuminated the heart of the God I was only just now beginning to believe existed. For the first time in my life, I heard the story of the Prodigal Son—and I immediately knew that this son was *me.*

"To become a Christian is not to accept a Western religion," Dr. Mooneyham said, "it is to come home."

I cried for the acceptance I now knew. I cried for my prodigal ways. I cried for my mistaken loyalties. And in my heart I ran home into the arms of my Father.

A childhood steeped in Buddhism had taught me discipline. Because I was my father's favorite son, he devoted much of his time to teach me the work ethic he embraced. Each night I was required to read a portion of Buddhist scriptures or a few chapters of a book my father selected. I read aloud, pausing whenever my father interrupted to correct my pronunciation. Every morning at 4:00 my father shook me awake and propped me, still heavy with sleep, on his shoulder. On his other shoulder he carried a basket. Together we walked to the paddy fields, where we collected *tanot-tom* (overripe sugar palm nuts) for the family's breakfast. My father had been a monk before he married his first wife. One of my brothers was a monk.

The first of Buddhism's "fourfold truths," the noble truth of suffering, was ingrained not only into my culture but also into my family's daily life. Hard work, our most familiar experience of suffering, was an accepted fact of our existence.

Buddhism also taught me a studied complacency toward life. All expressions of emotion were considered if not wrong, then weak. Desire was the very reason for suffering, so extremes of either were to be avoided. Although you could have easily called me a nominal Buddhist, I embraced the goal expressed in the fourth of the fourfold truths: "In order to enter into a state where there is no desire and no suffering, one must follow the true Way."

The Communists had seized these two ideals, the value of hard work and the degradation of desire, and pushed them to the extreme. During the years of the Killing Fields, work became the paramount virtue of the *Angkar*. It trumped everything personal, including love for family, affection, and emotion.

In 1972 I was fully committed to the self-control impressed upon me by my heritage and my political allegiance. And so, as I sat near the back in Chaktomuk Hall, I committed my first act of treason: I cried.

I cried for the acceptance I now knew—in contrast to this Father's love—I had never known. I cried for my prodigal ways. I cried for my mistaken loyalties. And in my heart I ran home into the arms of my Father.

Dr. Mooneyham invited us simply to ask Jesus into our hearts. He summoned those who responded to make their commitments public and walk to the front of the auditorium. Hundreds stood and made their way into the aisles and down to the front.

I would have done the same, but the aisles were clogged with people, many sobbing like me. I gave up and sat, very much a believer in Jesus but bewildered about what to do next. Two ushers came to me, knelt next to my seat, and asked if I was all right. Did I need anything? Through my tears, I told them I was ready to follow Jesus, but I didn't know what to do. These two men took my program and wrote the name and address of a church that met nearby. Not only was I now a son of a Father, but I also gained a new family.

Don't get me wrong. My birth family loved me, and I loved them. My Communist friends cared about me, and I cared about them. Mr. At Veth and I had a deep affection for one another. I knew my decision to become a Christian would cause him pain. I was young in years and now young in my faith, so I did what you would expect from an immature young man. I avoided him.

Written Proof

I immediately began to attend Bethany Church, the church the ushers had scrawled on my program. It was in the neighborhood of the *wat*, or Buddhist temple, where I lived. The elders at Bethany included Minh Thien Voan, the acting director of World Vision; Tan Van Jean, a banker; Nouth Chenda, a university lecturer; Chea Thai Seng, a dean at the Royal University of Fine Arts; and Men Ny Borin, a Supreme Court justice; and a host of other academics and professionals. With his position in the Supreme Court, Men Ny Borin enabled the church to obtain permits for baptisms, crusades, and other public events. In later chapters I will give brief histories of these men, many martyred during the Killing Fields.

The Communists often sang of brotherly love; we adopted each other as comrades in the cause. But now I was an adopted son of my Father. I had real, adopted brothers. While I sensed the difference right away, my family wasn't so easily convinced.

My father asked, "Son, why did you choose to become a Catholic?"

He thought all Christians were Catholics. Because of his memories of a Cambodia under French colonization, it was an understandable error. His recollections of Catholicism were not happy. During the ninety years before our country gained independence from France on November 9, 1953, some Cambodian Catholics interpreted Luke 14:26 literally: "If anyone comes to me and does not hate his own father and mother and wife and children and brothers and sisters, yes, and even his own life, he cannot be my disciple." My father heard the news of my conversion and braced himself for what he was sure would follow. He believed I would hate him.

My father confronted me with this question just six weeks after I committed my life to Christ. I had no idea how to answer him, so I asked the Holy Spirit to guide me.

"At church," I said, "I am taught to honor my parents."

"Really? Show this teaching to me in writing."

Again I prayed. And I breathed a thank-you to God for my new Bible. On my first visit to Bethany Church, I met Mr. Son Sonne of the Bible Society. I had been taught the British "Essential English" in school, but my ability to speak and read English with any real understanding was sorely limited. I told him I wanted a Bible and asked how I might get one when I had no money. He suggested I join him selling Bibles in front of the Royal Palace and in Wat Phnom Park on Sunday afternoons. He said I could earn enough on commission to buy my own Bible.

Close to five hundred people gave their lives to Christ during the first World Vision crusade that year, so Bibles were in high demand. On my first outing I earned enough money to buy a French Bible. Next I joined some students and sold enough Bibles to buy an English Bible. Finally, one week later, I earned enough to buy a Khmer Bible. On the front page of this Bible, I wrote: "Lord, grant me a favor. Make me a translator of the Bible and an interpreter of Your Word."

When my father asked for written proof, I had a book full of answers at my fingertips. I prayed again for the Holy Spirit's guidance and found the proof my father desired:

Honor your father and your mother, so that you may live long in the land the Lord your God is giving you. (Exodus 20:12 NIV)

Children, obey your parents in the Lord, for this is right. "Honor your father and mother"—which is the first commandment with a promise—"so that it may go well with you and that you may enjoy long life on the earth." (Ephesians 6:1–3 NIV)

In the face of such clear evidence that my new faith not only forbade me to hate them but rather instructed me to honor them, my father was satisfied. Both of my parents decided to tolerate my decision to follow Christ. Still, they wanted to know, "What are you going to do about your relationship with your brothers and sisters?"

Our family was large, and we had our share of jealousies and divisions. One sister had always resented the preferential treatment I received from our parents and older siblings. Once as I studied for an important exam, she moaned loudly in pain over a severe toothache, and I lost patience and spoke harshly to her. She responded by refusing to speak to me . . . for three years. Of course I didn't apologize or make any attempt to mend the relationship.

When my parents mentioned my siblings to me, I thought of this incident and how it related to a sermon I'd just heard.

"The Bible teaches us that reconciling with our brothers and sisters is vital," I said to my parents. "In fact, if we are about to leave a sacrifice at the altar and we remember that we've wronged someone, we should leave the sacrifice and go reconcile with that person. Only then can we return and make a proper sacrifice."

"Show this to us in writing," my wise parents said.

And so I did. I found Matthew 5:23–24 in my new Bible. But I also showed it to them in action. I asked my sister Rany for forgiveness, and she readily gave it. Our relationship was restored. And my parents saw the Word lived out in their own home.

Notes

1. Harriet Beecher Stowe, *Uncle Tom's Cabin* (Hertfordshire, London: Wordsworth Editions Limited, 2002), 293.

2. Mao Tse-Tung, *Quotations from Chairman Mao Tse-Tung,* China Books and Periodicals (Melbourne: 1990), 11–12.

3. "Mao Tse-Tung" BrainyQuote.com. Xplore Inc, 2011. 7 December. 2011. www.brainyquote.com/quotes/quotes/m/maotsetun115703. html.

Chapter Four

TEMPLE BOY MEETS THE TRUE GOD

From Buddhism to Communism to Christ

The first requisite for the happiness
of the people is the abolition of religion.

—Karl Marx

. . . it is helpful to remember that the
question of Christianity and culture
is by no means a new one.

—Richard Niebuhr, in *Christ and Culture*

We are hard pressed on every side,
but not crushed; perplexed, but not in despair;
persecuted, but not abandoned;
struck down, but not destroyed.

—2 Corinthians 4:8–9 NIV

LET JESUS feed you now."

My uncle, the venerable So Lun, greeted the news of my conversion to Christianity with these words.

Just because I lived in a Buddhist temple—*Wat Saravoan*—and just because I was a "temple boy" who worked under the tutelage of my uncle, a monk in that temple, did not mean I was a devout Buddhist. These were merely surface descriptions of my life. I had already joined the Maquis faction of Communist activists, a movement that decried Buddhism and everything it stood for.

But culturally speaking, I still honored the party line. I came from a Buddhist family. I worked in a Buddhist temple. In every way, except in my heart and mind, I was a Buddhist. That's just the way things were.

When I was 19, I moved from my family's village to Phnom Penh to live and work at the *wat* with my uncle, nine other monks, and thirty other temple boys. My job title was master of ceremonies. Every morning at five, I gathered the other boys and led them in chanting Buddha's *dharma*, or liturgy, for thirty minutes. I cleaned my uncle's room and washed his saffron robes.

Each morning my uncle, So Lun, gave me four small baskets, the *chansrak*, which I carried into the city to collect food, soup, dessert, and cash for the monks and the boys who lived in the temple. One house where I went to beg every day was the home of a famous Cambodian movie star, Pech Saleurn, and his wife, Vijaradany. Twice a week I cooked *bawbaw*, a rice porridge, and *char trakuon*, fried morning glory with black soybean, as breakfast for the monks and my colleagues.

After breakfast, the boys attended schools in the area, either high schools or colleges. At times I shadowed my uncle as he performed other duties in the community. He would visit new homes to pray for blessings on the family or sprinkle *mantra* (sacred) water over a home to purge it of bad luck. All over the country, routines like these dug into the soil of our culture. The ruts they created were centuries old.

Each *wat* was more than a place of worship. It was considered the cradle of civilization for the surrounding community. It housed the primary school and the hospital for traditional healing, and it served as the home of all spiritual leadership and wisdom. *Wat Saravoan* was located near the Royal Palace in Phnom Penh. Unlike the palace or the nearby "Silver Pagoda" with their ocher walls, majestic statues, and dainty, filigreed eaves, our *wat* was a simple, functional compound.

On the weekends I studied under several famous Buddhist scholars. As I worked for my uncle, he also invested a lot of his time and resources in me. I'm sure he thought that I, by embracing Christianity, had taken everything he poured into my life and discarded it. It must have felt like a slap in the face.

"Let Jesus feed you now," he said.

And then, for six weeks, he made good on that proposition.

East Meets West

When does a religion become a relic? How does it calcify in a way that no one notices until the entire structure is as hard as ancient statuary? When do the rituals slip from being fresh ideas, meant to serve people with a purpose, to become patterns people feel obliged to serve even though they cannot remember why?

We are called to
relate rightly to culture
—to not only preach salvation
but also to love in such a way
that our culture
is imprinted with that love.

Buddhism thrived in Cambodia before the Killing Fields, but a slow hardening had already begun. Everyone was just too comfortable in the rituals. The Communists accused the monks of parasitism, of living off of the labor of others. This accusation contained enough truth for those who were poor or oppressed to begin blaming the monks. One saying of the *Angkar*'s new religion was, "The monks use other people's noses to breathe. It is *Angkar*'s rule: Breathe by your own nose."[1]

Buddhist life in Cambodia, before the Khmer Rouge annihilated it, was a life where religion and everything else comingled fluidly. Buddha's image loomed large, as the cross of Christ once did in Western culture. It is a chilling déjà vu—this symbiotic bond between Cambodian religion and Cambodian culture—that, if we will let it, reminds the church to be wary of its own relationship to culture.

What exactly are the distinctive features of the church that transcend culture? How can we give to culture rather than simply mimic it? What is left when that culture is stripped away? And, if we lose it, will we be purified or destroyed? We must continually ask ourselves these questions. The church needs to ask them, not only to avoid the kind of violent political backlash we experienced in Cambodia but because we are called to relate rightly to culture —to not only preach salvation to the lost but also to love in such a way that our culture is imprinted with that love.

In their groundbreaking book *unChristian*, Dave Kinnaman and Gabe Lyons dare to wonder what has happened to Christianity's image in the United States.[2] The writers surveyed hundreds of unbelievers to understand their perceptions about the church. In their research Kinnaman and Lyons uncover this unsettling truth: Non-Christians in America don't trust Christians. And because they don't trust us, they don't trust our message.

Wait a minute, I thought we were talking about Buddhist culture. Yes, we were. But my skepticism about the cultural Buddhism of pre–Khmer Rouge Cambodia was uncannily similar to what I read in *unChristian*. In its pages, I hear my own voice.

At that time, before I met Christ, I represented an entire generation of young, educated Cambodians who were ready to discard their parents' traditional ways because those ways did not exhibit true compassion, nor did they stand up to critical thinking. The disillusionment is all too familiar.

The Narrow Place in the Hourglass

Much like many American believers, whose stories began in a nominally Christian environment, my life began in the context of Cambodian Buddhist culture. Try to picture the time line of my life from my days in the *wat* until the present as an hourglass: wide, then narrow, then wide once again. I started in the broad expanse of a country saturated with Buddhism.

My brief interlude in the Maquis encouraged me to question this culture, to poke holes in the reasoning behind its rituals, to notice the hypocrisy of its leaders, and ultimately to rebel against it. But I could not completely leave it because it was woven into the fabric of my everyday life. Still, in some ways you might say Communism prepared me to finally leave Buddhism for Christ.

Because God is a personal Father, the next chapter

of my story, the one where Jesus becomes my Lord, is intensely personal. Over time, my relationship with Christ caused my life to broaden, as all stories of this kind must. I began to hone the gifts that God would later use to impact others.

But then three years later, on April 17, 1975, my story narrowed to one of individual survival. Even so, the gospel is infectious. If we hear it and respond, it cannot remain personal and narrow. It defies boundaries. Even when my life seemed reduced to day-to-day subsistence, the gospel seeped out.

But it wasn't until my family escaped to Thailand and we began to plant churches there that my personal story widened again into one that influenced a people and a culture. It is as if God sifted me out of Cambodian culture, walked with me every step of a long season of suffering and loneliness, and then poured me back into that culture as a new man.

I memorized Psalm 23.
I learned the truth of the words,
"I shall not want."
But that was only a glimpse
of how faithfully
God would provide.

I have great respect for the many Buddhist monks who were martyred during those years. My uncle and my brother Sovannara number among them. Many were noble and sincere.

In discussing the deconstruction of Buddhism in Cambodia, I want to tread carefully. I can't be sure, but I wonder if one reason Buddhism in Cambodia faltered under fire is because it wasn't personal enough. It was a system, a tradition, an accepted way of life. But it wasn't a love affair between God and humanity. Can this also be true of Christianity when it devolves into a dry institution? When there remains nothing personal about it?

When I responded to the good news in 1972, I responded *personally* to the Word of God and to the Holy Spirit who made that Word real. This kind of intimacy—listening to my Lord speak and speaking back to Him—has endured in my relationship with Him. I only had three years to read and study the Bible before it was taken from me.

During those three years, I memorized Psalm 23. When my uncle refused to give me the food I earned in the *wat*, I learned the truth of the words, "I shall not want." My new Christian brothers and sisters saw to it that I didn't go hungry. But that was only a glimpse of how hungry I would become—and how faithfully God would provide for my needs.

The voice of God spoke those verses to me many

times during the years when no other voice spoke truth, when I was alone. When hunger, need, and danger dogged at my heels. When I lived at the narrowest place in the hourglass, God spoke them clearly, personally, to me.

The Valley of the Shadow of Death

Let's skip ahead for a moment to something that happened when I was in Sambok Moan, one of many prisons built during the first year of the Killing Fields. If the *cadres* wakened you late in the night, you assumed you were going to be tortured or killed. Twice every week, soldiers entered the hut where we prisoners lay side by side on connected bamboo cots. They called out the names of those who were due for *chivatuos*, a "self-assessment" session, then marched us into a courtyard for questioning.

These interrogations were like blindfolded trips through a minefield. Hidden meanings and trick questions kept us on our toes. There was no self-assessing during these encounters. It was brainwashing. And, if he gave any hint of rebellion against the *Angkar*, the prisoner who dared to answer for himself would be taken away. We all knew "Take him away" meant death. By then we also knew that any show of emotion was grounds for execution. The Communists were fond of saying, "Shed blood, not tears."

One night, I was summoned very late into the courtyard with a few other men. We huddled in a row, waiting our turn to answer questions. As I waited, preparing to be taken away, to be with the Lord, I murmured the words of Psalm 23. "The valley of the shadow of death" had become a familiar place. But the presence of the One who promised to be with me in that valley had become even more familiar.

The *cadres* dragged the first prisoner in line into the center of the courtyard for questioning. One other man stood between this prisoner and me. We weren't there just for our own interviews with the guards. We were there to be intimidated by the treatment of our cell mates. A *cadre* stood before the man and asked in a kind, soft voice, so low that we strained to hear, "Do you miss your wife and family?"

During those years, nothing was as it seemed. Although the *Angkar* proclaimed that all people were equal, it just wasn't so. In their army, the honor of one person over another was designated with subtle symbols. A young boy with no shoes might be a bodyguard with the privilege of shouldering a heavy AK-47. If a *cadre* rode a bicycle or wore sandals made from rubber tires, he was surely a team leader. The more pens a man had in his breast pocket, the higher his rank. A pen in the pocket meant that officer was authorized to kill anyone he pleased.

That night, the man who bent over the prisoner had a pen or two in his pocket. That also meant he was practiced in the art of Khmer Rouge mind games. As a young Communist, I'd had some experience with this kind of deception in our debates with potential recruits. Only now there was no debate.

The prisoner, I could tell, believed the *cadre* genuinely cared about him. His eyes flickered with the hope that someone with influence understood his plight, that he was about to be reunited with his family. He said, "Oh yes, *Comrade*, I do!"

"Take him away," the *cadre* said.

The prisoner had placed his life in this *cadre*'s hands. Execution was the price for that kind of trust.

The man standing by me was called to the center of the courtyard. I knew I would be next. I began to ask the Holy Spirit how I should answer. I had already determined to be honest. But how? My mind worked along two tracks. First, I told the Lord I was ready to be with Him. Second, I continued to observe the proceedings and asked for wisdom when my time came.

"Do you miss your wife and family?" the *cadre* asked again.

This time there was no pretense of concern. "Just answer the question," he said.

"Oh no, not at all," said the second man. He believed his unfortunate predecessor had given him a clue to the right answer.

"He is a liar," the *cadre* shouted, "take him away!"

I never saw either of these two men again.

It was my turn. One more time I breathed a prayer, asking the Holy Spirit to tell me what to say. "Do you miss your family?" the *cadre* asked with a cunning smile.

At that time, I was not officially married. The *cadre* clearly knew this about me since he did not ask about my wife. This subtle omission made his question more unnerving. He stared at me, as if he knew he had trapped yet another weak-minded prisoner.

"I am here," I said, "not to learn to miss my family but to learn to work as hard as I possibly can."

I had told the truth. I had also literally dodged a bullet. The God who promised to be with me in the lowest valley of the darkest shadow of death had rescued me.

God's Favor

Three years earlier, soon after I gave my life to Christ, several of my contemporaries in the Maquis came to visit me. Their agenda was transparent. They came to talk me out of my decision to follow Jesus. They even attended a Bible study with me, hoping to convince me of the folly of believing in a God they were persuaded did not exist. I was still a baby in the faith, but I knew there was a Creator God and that He loved me. I was already bound to Him by that love.

I told my friends that if they could present someone to me who would love and accept me like my God did, I would reconsider my decision. I asked them to search their experiences and their memories to see if a man or a woman existed who could love as wholly and as sacrificially as Jesus. I challenged them to name a being who was worthy of human worship, one who was perfect by every possible measure.

"Yes, we know of someone," they said, "and you do too."

I had not known the truth about God for long, but this I knew: no one loved me like He did. No one. I waited to hear what they would say.

"Mao Zedong!" they cried in uniso. "He is worthy."

My friends' answer only saddened me. Eventually they lived long enough for it to sadden them too. When all was stripped away, their human gods were exposed as frail, limited, imperfect beings. Their man-made system with all its corruption was likewise laid bare. All was stripped away and the tragic truth revealed: there was nothing there.

Earlier I asked, What is left for Christians when culture is stripped away? This remains a hypothetical question until we experience loss. And then we know the answer faith gave us before the loss. God remains.

I have many more stories that demonstrate God's favor in my life. Because I experienced such shocking loss, the stories shock as well. They are nothing short of miraculous. But I do not want to make God's favorable actions toward me—when I was in need—the focus of my story. They are not.

The central point of this drama is the God who shows favor, the God who walked with many of my brothers and sisters through the valley of the shadow of death and led them to a different destination from mine. They are now in His presence. They do not need the hope or the faith of which my story speaks. That's because, when all is gone, God remains—and what we'll see of Him most clearly in that day is His love.

> Now we see but a poor reflection as in a mirror; then we shall see face to face. Now I know in part; then I shall know fully, even as I am fully known. And now these three remain: faith, hope and love. But the greatest of these is love. (1 Corinthians 13:12–13 NIV)

Notes

1. Haing Ngor, *Survival in the Killing Fields* (New York: Carroll & Graf, 1987), 149.
2. Dave Kinnaman and Gabe Lyons, *unChristian* (Grand Rapids: Baker Books, 2007).

Chapter Five

A TALE OF
THREE KINGS

The Powerful
and the Powerless

The best way to convert a villager to Communism was
to burn his house down and kill one or more members
of his family. In this way you abolished a man's
inducement to lead a quiet, respectable existence.[1]

—Norman Lewis in *Dragon Apparent*

We have, I fear,
confused power with greatness.

—Stewart Udall

No, in all these things we are more
than conquerors through him who loved us.

—Romans 8:37 NIV

It is a shameful thing for a Christian to talk about
getting the victory. We should belong so completely
to the Victor that it is always His victory.

—Oswald Chambers

ONE WEEK after Phnom Penh's evacuation, Battambang, the second-largest city in Cambodia, was also purged of its inhabitants. Both cities disgorged their citizens with the force of one repeated threat: the American B-52 bombers were coming, the cities' people were told. Although the bombers didn't come, the threat was not empty. At Battambang, soldiers lynched the previous government's pilots. Then, all over Cambodia, the Khmer Rouge began the violent eradication of anyone who was in any way associated with those pilots, the planes they flew, and the bombs they dropped.

Over the next four years, Pol Pot's Democratic Kampuchea disassembled an entire nation. Within days all our cities hollowed out. Hospitals were emptied, schools closed, factories shut down, money eliminated, monasteries vacated, and libraries destroyed. All freedoms— even affection for family or conversation with friends —were abolished for the next four years. "A whole nation was kidnapped and then besieged from within."[2]

How many times in history have the oppressed become the oppressors? How many conflicts can be attributed to this cycle: the ruling power abuses that power, and the abused rise up only to wield power just as abusively?

Most of us have heard the quote, attributed to British historian Lord Acton, "Power corrupts and absolute power corrupts absolutely." Only the very young or the very naïve disagree. The powerful eventually devour the powerless. And power in the hands of those who were powerless a mere generation ago is the most dangerous of all. We see this fact played out in everyday life. The strong belittle the weak because of some hidden weakness of their own. The rich take advantage of the poor, especially the "new rich" who remember being poor. A child is bullied at home and becomes the bully on the playground. The pattern is as familiar as our childhoods.

Even so, a helpless wonder emerges in the souls of sane people when power goes berserk. The wholesale wielding of that power makes us stop and stare, like motorists slowing to gawk at a horrific accident. I think this is the ultimate impact of the Killing Fields on those who were there and upon those who have studied it from afar: we were too stunned to ask why. The immediate reaction was shock; the gradual one despair. If the powerful among us could do *this*, what hope is there for any of us?

But what if, in the perpetual clash between the weak and the powerful, there is room for hope? What if, regardless of how things look, the powerful never really win?

Three Kings

All dramas have a beginning and an end. Tragedies and mysteries alike keep us guessing about the plot and the true mettle of the characters until the final page. And so the story is never complete until the last word is written.

In history's tragic time lines, we—the ones who live on—sometimes wish we could reveal that last word before its time. We'd like to invite the powerful to preview their last days. Surely we could change history if we interrupted the beginning with a sobering look at the inevitable end. Show Napoleon a picture of his conquered troops at Waterloo. Give Hitler a glimpse of the smoke-filled bunker where he died. These leaders, and countless others, experienced a zenith in their rise to power. They each tasted victory. But in each case, the last word was defeat. And that final chapter gives their entire story its meaning. In the end, they did not win.

Three men shaped the destiny
of my country—and of my life.
But only one built a lasting empire.

Still, it is small comfort to know oppressors never win. Does a mother gain any solace from watching the execution of her child's murderer? Does an entire country heal simply because of a political power shift? History tells us it does not. Is punishment or banishment of one's enemies all there is to winning? Justice is important, but surely victory means more than this.

I'd like to redefine the word "victory" by telling you about three rulers. These three men shaped the destiny of my country—and of my life. These three kings built empires, but only one built a lasting one.

Suryavarman II

Angkor Wat, a vast temple complex in the forests of Cambodia, was erected early in the twelfth century by a Khmer king named Suryavarman II. The *wat*, now partially in ruins, was designed to represent the fictional Mount Meru of Hindu mythology. Like Mount Olympus in Greek mythology, Meru was considered the home of the Hindu deities. The king used its many stone carvings as an everlasting reminder of his supposed divinity.

Although he called himself "Lord of the Universe," Suryavarman was keenly aware that his divinity wasn't assured; it was fragile and had to be maintained. Thus the temple complex, a marketing tool for the king's assertion of divinity, was regularly expanded until it reached gargantuan proportions. Including the outer wall, *Angkor Wat* covers nearly two hundred acres. It is so large, all the monuments of ancient Greece could fit into it.[3]

Suryavarman built his kingdom and his claims of deity on the backs of the peasant class.

On one of *Angkor Wat*'s steles, a later king suggests that the immortality of the king was dependent upon the support of the regional Hindu cult, which later evolved into Buddhism. In one of the carvings, the Churning of the Sea of Milk, eighty-eight *asuras* (demigods, demons) and ninety-two *devas* (gods) stir the ocean to extract the elixir of immortality. Clearly, becoming a god took some effort.

The area was abandoned by the Khmer people in the 1500s when Thailand invaded and drove them south toward Phnom Penh. All that we know of Suryavarman comes from the buildings at *Angkor Wat.* The man himself passed into oblivion centuries ago. The empire he built followed suit. All that is left of the Khmer king who sought to be a god are perishable sandstone structures, some still standing and some in piles of rubble.

Considered the biggest religious monument on earth, *Angkor Wat* is a Cambodian national treasure. Archaeologists believe it was the largest preindustrial city in the world. In the last few years several forces have conspired to further its decay, prompting a massive, ongoing renovation effort that began in 1986. First, like most abandoned areas, looting has always been a problem. Second, the two million visitors who tour *Angkor Wat* every year have created a host of environmental issues that damage the area and the buildings.

Finally, as you would expect after eight hundred years, the jungle has encroached into *Angkor Wat*'s territory. It is amazing that both entities have coexisted for so long. One—the jungle—an undeniable declaration of God's

creative power. The other—Suryavarman's temple city—
a crumbling statement of man's power. Could it be that
every conflict on earth, whether slight or significant, is a
reflection of these two powers colliding? If so, Suryavarman never had a chance. Neither did Pol Pot.

Pol Pot

Before 1975, Cambodia's population was 80 percent
peasant, 80 percent Khmer, and 80 percent Buddhist.
These figures suggest a country that was more homogeneous than most. But homogeneous is not the same as co-
hesive. Our villages, though ethnically and educationally
uniform, existed as disconnected entities. Our small
urban population lived as a separate society from the
peasant class.

The Khmer Rouge eventually rolled all Communist
factions into one. They then divided Cambodia into seven
zones. The communication between people in these re-
gions was poor, the conflict between them palpable, and
their inability to trust each other bordered on paranoia.

Perhaps this is why, when we were driven from Phnom
Penh, the process was so chaotic. The soldiers who barked
orders in the streets gave conflicting information. Some
said we could pack our things; others said we could not.
Some said we would be gone three hours; some three
days. Some were kind to the evacuees when they balked
at leaving; others shot them for the smallest provocation.

At every turn, the *Angkar* contradicted itself.

Ninety years of French colonial rule (1863–1953) had encouraged isolation from our neighboring countries of Laos, Thailand, and Vietnam. From the time of his birth in 1928, Saloth Sar (later known as Pol Pot) lived just such an isolated life. He was born in a thriving peasant village to a landowner who, with his sons and adopted nephews, grew enough rice for about twenty people. Although they were more affluent than their neighbors, the family participated in all the same activities and no one considered them outsiders.

But Pol Pot was destined to live outside village life. His family had ties to King Monivong's palace, and when he was six years old, Pot joined his brother Saloth Suong, who was a consort there. He spent a year in the royal monastery and then six years in *Ecole Miche*, an elite Catholic school. Palace life was sequestered, just the place to develop utopian ideas about society without any real connection to that society. In 1948, Pot won a scholarship to study radio electronics in Paris. There, during the height of Stalin's popularity in Europe, he joined the French Communist Party.

Pol Pot returned to Cambodia in January 1953, after failing his final exam for the third time. Just days before he arrived, Prince Sihanouk had declared martial law to suppress the growing independence movement (Sihanouk garnered independence for our country just two years later).

Pot, along with his brother Saloth Chhay joined the Vietnamese and Cambodian Communists. During this time he began to form the strong opinion that "everything should be done on the basis of self-reliance, independence, and mastery. The Khmers should do everything on their own."[4] Although he had elite training overseas, Pot never achieved a leadership position in this group. It's hard to miss the connection between what he surely perceived as a slight by the Vietnamese Communists and Pot's fierce desire to separate from them.

Long before Pol Pot's separatist ideas emerged, the nationalism that drew me into the Maquis had begun to brew throughout the country. In 1942, a decade before Cambodia gained its independence from France, two Buddhist monks were arrested for preaching nationalist sermons. As a result, seven hundred monks protested in Phnom Penh, joined by two thousand civilians. The French police responded by arresting the leaders, but more always filled their places.

Two of these former monks, Son Ngoc Minh and Tou Samouth, participated in the riots and later joined Ho Chi Minh's Indochina Communist Party. They essentially began the independence movement and formed a viable Communist Party in Cambodia comprised of former monks and peasants. On one side this growing movement prompted Prince Sihanouk, a brilliant diplomat, to move toward middle ground and promote neutrality. On the other it provided a platform for Pol Pot to fuel the spreading fire of insurgency.

Several key things happened as this nationalist flame burned hotter. First, Cambodia's leading Communists, who had been rural, Buddhist, and pro-Vietnam, became urban, educated, and anti-Vietnam. Second, Prince Sihanouk, after being ousted by Lon Nol, aligned himself with the only other power in the country, the Communists. Finally, the radicalism of Pol Pot's Communists increased and the *Angkar* began to eclipse or destroy all other factions.

The fate of one of Pol Pot's early colleagues foreshadows his march toward maniacal despotism. Hou Yuon was a popular intellectual among the Cambodian Marxists who studied in Paris. Even in those years, he was not one to toe the party line. He was a charismatic and opinionated insider among Pol Pot's circle of friends. The two men remained politically connected in various ways until April 17, 1975.

Yuon opposed the evacuation of Phnom Penh and the other cities. He felt it was too radical and too soon. He did not keep his opinion to himself—not the first time Yuon expressed reservations about Khmer Rouge tactics. No one knows precisely what happened to Hou Yuon. Some reports say he committed suicide in prison. Others believe he was executed. Either way, he disappeared—the movement's first upper-echelon casualty.

If Hou Yuon, a party insider, could lose favor so quickly for daring to express hesitation about an *Angkar* decision, you can only imagine how Pol Pot felt about the Americans. Sadly, the US intervention inside our borders during the sixties and early seventies—which often translated into civilian deaths—is considered by many to be "the most important single factor in Pol Pot's rise."[5]

American support of Lon Nol was not merely diplomatic. Many Cambodians who joined the Communists during those years can trace their shift in political allegiance to specific events, such as an aerial assault that took the lives of fifty villagers, another attack that claimed seven in one family, or the casualties near the border where minefields carpeted the land.

US Green Beret Special Forces, called Daniel Boone teams, infiltrated the country, planting minefields as they went. In the year before Lon Nol's coup of Sihanouk's government, more than 3,600 B-52 bombing raids took place. About 100,000 *tons of bombs* were dropped in missions that were code-named "Menu" with targets that were labeled "Breakfast, Snack, Lunch, Dinner, Dessert, and Supper."[6] These examples—and more—provided the Khmer Rouge ammunition for a different kind of firepower: propaganda. Pol Pot had only to point to the American-induced losses of our own people to enlist angry recruits and to excuse the violent nature of his own policies.

Such were the ashes of our country from which Pol Pot rose to power in 1975. Hou Yuon is said to have predicted, "If you go on like this, I give your regime three years. Then it will collapse."[7] He was very nearly right. Pol Pot's victory was short-lived. But, while it lasted, it was a victory.

Pol Pot and the Khmer Rouge simply perpetuated a cycle that is older than the crumbling ruins of *Angkor Wat*. They used their power to leverage the anger of the peasant class. For a season—long enough to claim the lives of nearly two million people—mayhem and murder prevailed. Pol Pot called 1975 "Year Zero" because of his plan to restart civilization in Cambodia. His troops marched into Phnom Penh and defeated Lon Nol's army, but neither the haves nor the have-nots gained anything. The rebuilding of society never took place. Cambodia became a vast field of plowed land with nothing of value planted in the deep furrows of the Khmer Rouge "victory."

The King of Glory

We Christians talk a lot about victory. We sing about it. We "claim" it over enemies like addiction or adversity. In the West this Christian concept of victory seems to make sense. It resonates in the American Dream. But in my part of the world, it is a little harder to understand.

Everything about our recent history in Cambodia echoes with defeat. Yet 2 Corinthians 2:14 appears to promise we'll always win: "But thanks be to God, who in Christ always leads us in triumphal procession." What does that really mean? Does it mean Christians will triumph in every arena of life, from parking our cars in convenient spots to conquering disease? Or is it some ethereal, spiritual ideal that has no bearing on everyday life? Is victory an ancient truth, a future hope, or a present reality? And what impact does the struggle between God's preeminent power and the power of, well, everything else have on us? What part do we play?

As you read on, you'll hear about my personal victories. You'll see that God won in my own heart *during* bouts with sin, sickness, emotional distress, and sorrow. I hope these stories encourage you in your own circumstances. But I'm not sure this is an adequate picture of God's power—or His victory.

Victory is much bigger than the wildest story I could tell about my own life. Both Suryavarman and Pol Pot believed victory and the power to get it were theirs for the taking. But even for the rulers of earth's strongest nations, power has never been a human commodity to be bought or won. It doesn't belong to us. And if it did, we couldn't handle it. It is too big. It is as big as God Himself. It is as big as His glory.

It is supremely ironic that I learned the most about power when I was the most powerless. This story happened during the eleven months it took my family and me to escape to Thailand. I had already lived as a prisoner and a slave to the Khmer Rouge for four years. I then became a worship leader in the underground church in Phnom Penh, which meant I could be arrested any day.

God would indeed
wield His power on my behalf,
but not just to make my life easier.
I could count on Him to lead me
"for His name's sake."

I had not lived what anyone would consider a victorious life. But the truths in Psalm 23 had become more real to me than the *kramar* I wore every day around my neck. Those truths taught me both the present reality—"He leads me in paths of righteousness"—and the future promise—"Surely goodness and mercy shall follow me all the days of my life." I was secure in these promises, so secure I usually expected God's goodness rather than praying for it.

I had also begun to realize that this "path of righteousness" had a purpose that stretched far beyond my own comfort and well-being. God would indeed wield His power on my behalf, but not just to make my life easier.

I could count on Him to lead me "for His name's sake." Second Corinthians 2:14 describes the Christian's life as a "triumphal procession," one where we are followers in the train of our victorious Lord. It isn't our victory; it is His.

But many times life does not seem like a triumphal procession. When my family decided to leave Phnom Penh and escape to Thailand, we made what we believed were wise plans.[8] I would leave first, alone. Then one month later my stepdaughter Kanika would leave, followed yet another month later by another stepdaughter, Sokunaroat. Lastly, my wife, Boury, and our daughter, Shalom, who was then only four, would leave. Traveling separately was the only way to avoid suspicion. We thought it would take about three months. It ended up taking almost a year.

With two friends I set off for Sihanoukville on the southern coast of the Gulf of Thailand. One was my step-son-in-law, a low-ranking officer in the new army; the other was a guitarist. My musician friend and I borrowed military uniforms so all three of us looked like soldiers. We took a flute and a guitar and hoped anyone who asked would believe we were going to Sihanoukville to perform in a concert. A friend who held a local administrative office in Phnom Penh issued us each travel documents with different identities. We left early in the morning, riding in a military truck that doubled as a taxi. Many bridges were down, and the roads were bumpy and often blocked. A four-hour trip took us the entire day.

From Sihanoukville, we went to a nearby fishing village in the Stung Hao district, where we visited the home of a friend who was an authority in the city. He knew we were planning to escape. But when we arrived, we were greeted by local agents who had noticed us in Sihanoukville and followed us. My friend vouched for us, and the agents left. I said we were interested in visiting the village of Laem Son, where my brother Samon's widow and her three sons lived.

"Don't worry," my friend said. "I'll organize everything for you. Just enjoy your lunch, and by nightfall a fishing boat will be ready."

As planned, my musician friend and I parted ways with my stepson-in-law. At dusk the two of us rode on the back of our host's Honda through the hills to another fishing village called Kampenh where we met his brother-in-law, Mee, a well-to-do man who was respected by everyone—police officers, government officials, even the district governors. Mee and I had known each other since childhood. I trusted him. The fishermen in this part of Cambodia are typically more affluent than those in other areas. Most families own more than one boat, which they use for fishing and for importing goods from Thailand into Cambodia. For a Cambodian to have options economically at that time was incredibly rare.

Mee asked us to wait one more day for a bigger boat so he could guarantee our safety to Laem Son. But I was impatient. We were so close, I argued, we should leave that very night. Mee arranged for us to depart in a small fishing boat. As we were waiting for darkness to fall, the weather began to change rapidly. Again, Mee advised against traveling. And again I urged him to take us that night. Against his counsel, my friend and I bid Mee good-bye and left for Laem Son with his elderly father in the smaller boat. We did not make it to our destination that night, but the storm wasn't the reason why.

Soon after we departed, we passed an island. In the pitch black we heard a voice shout in Vietnamese, "Stop!" followed by gunshots. At the time the Vietnamese navy contracted with our government to patrol these waters. We knew the next shot would be aimed at us, so we landed on the small island and allowed ourselves to be taken by the marine guard. All I could think about was what I knew would come next: interrogation and arrest. The future I anticipated and the fear it produced were all too familiar.

The guard took us back to Sihanoukville where we were escorted to a temporary security checkpoint that had been set up in an old oil refinery. There were more than a hundred people detained in this cavernous facil-ity. My wife had an aunt who worked in Sihanoukville, so I began to ask everyone if they knew her. I sent a message to ask her to come visit me, hoping she would act as my advocate. At first she didn't come because she didn't recognize the false identity I still used. Eventually, she came. She wanted to help but couldn't.

"I have just returned from Phnom Penh where I stayed one week longer than I was allowed to stay," she said. "I am in trouble with the authorities now."

"I understand," I said, "but would you do me one favor? Would you get word to Boury that I've been arrested and ask her to pray for me?"

"That is the one thing I *can* do." That day she sent a letter to Boury by taxi.

That night I prayed, "Lord, deliver me from the interrogators. Release me in such a way that I will never face imprisonment again. I ask for freedom to go to Thailand so I can serve You by building Your church there and lead Your people to worship You."

The next morning my friend and I were taken to be questioned. We sat across a table from one security officer who was flanked by a row of gunmen. We answered questions for hours. Our interrogator suspected we were escaping to Thailand, so I told him the truth. "Yes, if there is a way, I will go to Thailand. If not, I'll stay in Laem Son with my sister-in-law and her children."

Before the officer could respond, we heard a crash followed by shouts. Someone came to the door and called the men outside. The sound was a train hitting a car. My friend and I were left alone. I wondered aloud whether we should run. Because I had prayed so specifically the night before, I sensed something miraculous would happen. I didn't want to miss what God would do, so we sat and waited until the officer returned, about thirty minutes later. Besides, we knew running would only result in arrest and more trouble.

The officer sat down before us, the notes he had been taking still in his hand. He looked into my eyes. "Why did you tell me the truth? No one has ever admitted that they are escaping to Thailand. No one. You are the two most foolish men on earth."

"Officer, I know you are very wise. If I tried to trick you with false answers, it wouldn't work. I knew this about you, so last night I prayed that a man like you would understand my situation and have pity on me. I know you will have mercy and not arrest me."

"You're right, I did not arrest you. You were arrested by the marine guard. My job is to interrogate you and give a report to the higher officials." He looked at us with an expression of wonder. "Don't worry. Just thirty minutes ago I ran into someone from the fishing village you sailed from. He is a commune leader there. I asked him if he knew you and your friend Mee whose father accompanied you in the boat. He said he did, and he pleaded with me to release you. I told him I could not without an official petition. He promised to send such a petition if I would go ahead and set you free. You're free to go."

The officer had one more thing to tell us. "Last night, after you were arrested, the storm got much worse. Even seasoned fishermen were taken by surprise, and many boats were caught in the storm. Many people lost their lives. It was a blessing that you were arrested. Now go in peace."

As we left for Laem Son, I sensed we were in that triumphant procession Paul talks about. Jesus Christ was the victor, we were His followers, and the promised "goodness and mercy" were not far behind. Was I reunited yet with my family? No. Was I out of danger? Definitely not. Was my life easy, predictable, or comfortable? Not at all.

But I had a song to sing that would soon resound in the hearts of the broken, the needy, and the outcasts in the largest refugee camp in Thailand. The Cambodian and Vietnamese people, who gathered by the thousands, would soon catch a hint of the aroma of Christ. Many would be ready to follow Him, and I would be there to show the way. God had opened a "path of righteousness for His name's sake." That's the kind of victory that endures for eternity.

Notes

1. Norman Lewis, *A Dragon Apparent: Travels in Cambodia, Laos & Vietnam* (London: Eland Publishing, 1951), 214.

2. Ben Kiernan, *The Pot Pot Regime: Race, Power, and Genocide in Cambodia under the Khmer Rouge*, 1975–79 (Chiang Mai, Thailand: Silkworm Books, 2005), 25.

3. Lewis, 232.

4. Kiernan, 12.

5. Kiernan, 16.

6. Seymour Hersh, *Price of Power: Kissinger in the Nixon White House* (New York: Summit Books, 1983), 177–78.

7. David Chandler, "Hou Yuon," Online Encyclopedia of Mass Violence. www.massviolence.org/Hou-Yuon.

8. By this time my common-law wife, Thavy, and I were no longer together. God blessed me with my wife, Boury, after the Killing Fields.

Chapter Six

THREE MOUNTAINS

But Only One Rock

"You must maintain a revolutionary attitude, and you must keep your mind on the guiding principles, the 'Three Mountains.' They are: 'Attain independence-sovereignty.' That is the first principle.
'Rely on our own strength.' That is the second.
And 'Take destiny into our hands.' "[1]

—The *Mit Neary* (female *cadres*) of the Khmer Rouge

For he will hide me in his shelter in the day of trouble;
he will conceal me under the cover of his tent;
he will lift me high upon a rock.

—Psalm 27:5

No one is as capable of gratitude as one who
has emerged from the kingdom of night.

—Elie Wiesel, Nazi Holocaust survivor

T**HE NAME** of the camp nestled in the rain forest near the Vietnam border, Sambok Moan, means "The Hen's Nest." But there was nothing there to suggest a mother hen or a nurturing nest. It was where I began to expect death. Even to welcome it.

More people died than lived at Sambok Moan. If the *cadres* called your name, you knew what was coming. If the call came early in the evening, you might survive the "self-assessment session" to which you were conveyed. If it came late at night, you gave your only shirt to a friend. You would never need it again.

The Khmer Rouge not only interrogated us over and over at Sambok Moan, they also pounded their doctrine into our heads. They never let us forget the agenda. We soon realized the real dogma—one more memorable than "The Three Mountains" or the hundreds of slogans that were just those same "mountains" modified to suit the occasion. The final word of *Angkar* was this: hunger, sickness, toil, and the inevitability of a painful death.

For nine months these were my daily truths at Sambok Moan, truths that seemed etched into the stone of my existence. Yet other, better, *more-true* truths began to fill my days: God is good and faithfully so. He speaks. He sustains. He lives. It has been more than three decades since Sambok Moan, and these are the truths that remain. Even then, when everything around me seemed to negate Him, God stood firm, firmer than any mountain.

Wanderings

There is much more to tell about those first nomadic weeks in 1975. Not many days after we were driven from Phnom Penh, all but one of my seventeen traveling companions left me. I didn't blame them. Like me, they were looking for their families. Their search led them in a different direction, by boat up the Mekong River. My friend Song and I continued the search for our own families on foot. For the next two months, from daybreak to sunset, we continued our pilgrimage from village to village, covering about forty miles every day on National Road Number One. We were never really alone. Others shuffled along every main road that led away from Phnom Penh, and we saw our fellow travelers grow more malnourished, tired, and ill before our eyes. Like the war-ravaged countryside around us with the trees shorn of their foliage, the Cambodian people began shedding everything—bundles of provisions, old or sick family members—all but the barest necessities.

Although I didn't know it at the time, God had used both my family and my new Christian friends to prepare me to survive the trials to come.

Although I didn't know it at the time, God had used both my family and my new Christian friends to prepare me to survive the trials to come. I had spent the past three years developing relationships with the other believers in the city, and I considered them family too. After my conversion I stayed in my uncle's *wat* for a few months until a new friend, who played guitar at Bethany Church, invited me to live with his family. This man, Chhawn, was Song's brother-in-law. I also became friends with Minh Thien Voan, the acting director of World Vision. Minh offered me a job at the World Vision office as a warehouse manager. I was later promoted to the relief office and eventually to the accounting office.

Minh not only gave me a job, he also helped me refine my command of the English language by studying the book of John with me. World Vision offered a program, called "Practice Your English," for students with leadership potential. I qualified for the program and my English continued to improve. I met a Christian and Missionary Alliance missionary named Ruth Patterson who challenged me to study nursing in order to practice my English further. Ruth encouraged me to read through the Psalms in six months, and so I read one every morning and evening for the better part of a year.

When Song and I wandered the Cambodian countryside together, I had been a Christian for only three years. Yet I already carried a rich heritage of faith, thanks to the investment into my life by more mature believers. God had prepared me for what was to come. And He used my entire life, not just the three years following my conversion, to prepare me for His work. Nothing was wasted in His hands. The little bit of training I had in nursing complemented the rural healing skills I had learned from my father—wisdom as ancient as the local herbs he used to care for the people in our village. I had learned to cook from my sisters and in *Wat Saravoan*. Many city dwellers did not know how to prepare even the simplest food—and suffered as a result. And though it had become a dangerous skill to possess, I knew enough English to prove useful when the time came.

In our wanderings Song and I eventually ran into Chhawn and other members of his family at the Bassac River. They asked me to join them, but their family was heading north, and I didn't have a peace about going that way. I knew I would hurt them if I didn't stay, so after three days Song and I left secretly at midnight. I never saw Chhawn again. His entire family, except for his infant son, was killed by the Khmer Rouge. Chhawn's crime? He wore eyeglasses.

From the Bassac River we walked about forty miles to a small town on the Lower Mekong River. I had almost given up hope that I would find my family—or anyone I knew. Still, scanning the crowd of people in each village for a familiar face had become habitual. It was something you saw everyone doing those days. We were a nomadic mass of missing persons, all longing to find someone, anyone we knew. I arrived at dusk and began to look for a place to settle for the night. As the clearing in the village began to dim, the face I saw took my breath away. It was Thavy, a woman I knew quite well.

Marriage

My romance with Thavy began in 1970 in Kampong Phnom, where her father was the principal of the elementary school. He had been my teacher when I was young. Thavy and I were young, she was beautiful, and I was smitten. But it wasn't meant to be. She married someone else, and I moved on. But Thavy's marriage was disastrous. She and her husband divorced in 1974, and she later attempted suicide. When we met again, that same year, she was seeing a counselor and doing much better. She started attending my church, and our romance slowly began to rekindle. Then the evacuation extinguished every flame of new beginnings in everyone's lives. After I left Phnom Penh, I assumed I would never see Thavy again.

To understand what happened next, you must realize how desperate the times were—and how the Khmer Rouge treated marriage. To them it was a joke. A really bad joke that they played on all of us.

In several locations throughout the country, the *Angkar*

staged large, communal weddings. Brides and grooms were hastily chosen for each other by the *cadres*, married in a civil ceremony, then, in some cases, immediately executed. Between 1975 and 1979, close to one thousand couples were united by the Khmer Rouge. "In these 'weddings,' traditional ceremonies were banned; instead, couples vowed to accept each other and work to achieve the objectives of the revolution."[2] The rumors of arranged marriages circulated first; the horror of the executions came later.

Thavy had traveled to Kampong Phnom to live with her family in their ancient home. Many Cambodians sought the homesteads their families had claimed for centuries in the hopes they would find each other and be secure there. Thavy's father assumed she would be safe if she were already married. He came to me soon after I arrived and asked if I would marry her. He feared the *Angkar* would force her to marry someone she did not love and, more importantly, someone who would not love and care for her as he knew I would.

What we did not know at the time was that no one was safe. Marriage, whether coerced by the Khmer Rouge or established between two people who were committed to one another, meant nothing. It was neither honored nor protected.

When Thavy's father proposed this plan, I was reluctant. I still loved her, but there was no way to marry

her legitimately. In our culture, the involvement and blessing of parents and extended family is essential for a true
marriage. Our traditional marriage ceremony lasts three
days. Under the circumstances there was no way to follow
any of these regulations. If I agreed, we would not be truly
married.

I asked Thavy's father to give me some time to think
and pray. I had no one to consult but the Lord. That night,
I stood alone on the banks of the Lower Mekong and
prayed. I had never been more confused or lonely. The
moonlight didn't illuminate matters; the only thing the
full moon shone upon were the corpses—too many to
count—that floated one after another from Phnom Penh
to the Mekong Delta.

I had no peace about it, but I decided to become
Thavy's common-law husband despite my misgivings.
The next day, a friend who was a commander in the
Khmer Rouge army came to the village. He pulled me
aside and warned, "Do not stay where people know you.
The farther you travel, the safer you'll be. At least cross
the river."

I now journeyed with Thavy and her family. We secured a boat and began our journey up the Tonle Toch,
a small river that connects the Lower and Upper Mekong
Rivers, until we landed in a small village called Banteay
Dek. We were immediately cautioned to move on. "Moving on" meant a repeat of the day before: I waded into

the Tonle Toch up to my neck and towed the boat filled with Thavy and twenty of her family members upstream. We had heard the fishing was good in Banteay Dek, so staying there was a temptation. But safety was more urgent than a full stomach. So once again I became a human towboat and pulled us up the river to the township of Prey Veng.

Arrest

The day Pol Pot seized our cities, every citizen of Cambodia, with the exception of the few who comprised the Khmer Rouge, were placed under a sinister sort of house arrest. The "great leap forward" could not take place without forced labor.

The rhetoric of the *Angkar*, words we heard in every village and town, always glorified work. Their sayings combined a stringent work ethic with military language, so every kind of labor became a "great struggle" against the elements and the many problems associated with farming. "We were to 'struggle to cultivate rice fields vigorously', 'struggle to dig canals with great courage', 'struggle to clear the forest', and even 'struggle to solve the manure problem.'"[3]

At Prey Veng we again heard the message we had been hearing since we left Phnom Penh: leave the city and go out into the countryside. We were continually herded about like sheep. Sometimes we were given reasons for the constant relocating. Sometimes we were just expected to move when we were told. At Prey Veng we could do nothing but obey orders. We followed the herd to a small village near the Vietnam border where my friends' advice proved to be very wrong.

As Thavy's family and I continued on this nomadic drive, I began to piece together the tenets of Communism I had learned in the Maquis along with the insanely twisted version preached by the *Angkar*. We were hungry, weary, and numb, so the constant indoctrination didn't always sink in. Part of this indoctrination included the way people were organized. Overall, there were considered to be two groups of people: the new and the old. Because I was educated and lived in the city, I was a "new" person. The "old" people were those from the villages, simple people.

There was also another general division between us: the revolutionary (the Khmer Rouge) and the liberated (the people they had "freed" from Lon Nol). These were loose designations that could be manipulated to either protect or condemn. A villager who became a spy or a soldier for the local *cadres* was both "old" and "revolutionary." Because he fell into these two amoebic categories, he was given license to kill anyone he considered "new" or "liberated."

Our exodus began to take on a shaky sense of order as we settled into villages and the party leaders who commandeered those villages put us to work. Then the categories got more specific. All of Cambodia was divided into three "forces." Force Number One was made up of workers in the fields. Our five main crops were rice, corn, cassava, sweet potato, and tobacco, and we were all expected to plant and harvest as a collective workforce. Force Number Two consisted of the children, and Force Number Three included the sick or elderly. Neither of these groups was expected to work.

Villages became closely monitored communes, where our rations were commensurate with our force levels. Number One got the largest portion and Number Three the least. But even this arrangement depended on the supply (which never met the demand) and the generosity of the *cadres* (who usually fed themselves while we went hungry).

Under these conditions I was surprised the first time I was arrested. The morning after our arrival in the village near Prey Veng, I was approached by a *cadre* who told me I was being sent to a reeducation camp. I could not picture a camp with less freedom, less grueling work, and less regimentation than what I observed in the village.

Anxious to be well-prepared, I asked the *cadre* how I was going to study without any books or paper or pencils. He said something I had heard before, "Don't worry, the *Angkar* will provide." That should have been my clue. Had the *Angkar* made good on any of their promises?

Prisons on the Way to Prison

The immediacy of my arrest was breathtaking. One minute I was detained and the next we were leaving for Don Koeng, a house with only eighteen prisoners on the way to Sambok Moan. The night before, in Prey Veng, I discovered I had an old friend in the village. At the time, Chhae was in her seventies (she died in 2010 at the age of 108). Even then, she was a wise, older woman who cared for me. Later, after my imprisonment, she became my second mother. She knew I was about to be led away, so she boldly approached the *cadre* who arrested me.

"Yes, Mae Chhae?" ("Mae" means mother in Khmer and was a term of high respect among the Khmer Rouge.)

Chhae echoed the *cadre*'s deferential tone. "May I speak with the captive before you leave?"

"Of course."

Muteness became our collective state of being. It was safer to stay silent than to speak.

Chhae whispered to me, "Vann, you must learn to plant a *kapok* [cotton] tree."

It was an old Cambodian maxim, one I immediately understood. Planting a kapok tree means to be mute, to keep secrets. Chhae was not instructing me to lie, but she was telling me to keep my mouth shut.

Muteness became our collective state of being. Either by observing the torture of others or experiencing it ourselves, we became a voiceless people. It was safer to stay silent than to speak. Many learned this lesson the hard way. But I believe the Lord saved my life through Chhae's sage advice. She took the colossal risk to talk to me, and I was forewarned that talk was not worth the risk.

If the *cadres* respected Chhae for her age, they suspected me because of my youth. As the youngest prisoner at Don Koeng, I was considered the most dangerous. I was not allowed to work in the fields with the others for fear I would escape. At all times I was guarded by two gunmen. This actually worked in my favor. The two men pitied me, assuming I would die soon, so they gave me good food to eat. They even took me to their base camp, something prisoners were forbidden to see. Such knowledge marked me for certain death. But by then I had spent so much time in the company of these two men, they became my friends. I began to realize God's favor might come in unexpected packages.

In Don Koeng I learned skills that would later prove useful. We demolished a building and moved it, piece by piece, across a lake to another location. This is something the Khmer Rouge did repeatedly for no apparent purpose. Sometimes the only perceivable reason for a task was that it tested the prisoners.

We later tilled the land with a wooden plow, but no plowshare. The *Angkar* repeatedly put us in impossible situations that tested our strength and commitment. Asked if I could drive an oxcart, I replied that I could try. I did so, quite successfully. Eventually my command of these skills assured the *cadres* I was not the son of a rich man. How else would I know how to do such manual labor?

When the *Angkar* determined a new bridge was needed at Alok Dam nearby, I was selected for the work. During this time, I continually prayed for the skills to do whatever work was required of me. I also looked for opportunities to take initiative. I had read about farming in China's Cultural Revolution. Following their example, I mixed human waste and mud, dried it in the sun, and pounded it into "number one fertilizer." The guards praised such enterprise if it benefited the community. When possible I caught fish for the cooks to prepare for the guards. These skills eventually shattered the suspicions of my captors.

Next we prisoners were relocated to Chaeng T'ngai, nearer the Vietnam border. There were now sixty-eight of us. It was November, and the river near the prison camp was deep and cold. Our primary task was mending the road. We were told we would be released when the road was finished. Of course we never finished. And we were not released. The ground was frozen, our tools were severely inadequate, and our progress was slow.

Comrade Yem, one of the *cadres*, taunted me every day as I bent over my work. "Loser!" he would yell. "You are good for nothing."

He called me names that aren't suitable for print. My parents had been soft-spoken and kind. I had never been spoken to that way in my life. I was hungry, cold, tired, and in pain. Finally, one day I just couldn't take it, and I began to cry.

Considering the Communist stance toward any display of emotion, I might as well have tried to escape. Tears were strictly forbidden. After releasing my sorrow, I felt a little bit better, but now the officer could add this accusation to his litany of abuse, "I see you still bear the mark of capitalism."

A few days later, I fainted. As I chopped the unyielding ground, the hoe missed its mark and hit my left ankle, causing it to bleed continually. I don't know if it was the cold, the blood loss, or the pain, but I passed out.

When I came to, the guards were holding me upside down, dunking my head like a mop in a pail of freezing water. The guards packed tobacco into the open wound and secured it tightly with a bandage of ragged cloth. It was a very painful treatment, but somehow it worked. After that my nemesis, Mit Yem, changed his attitude toward me. He never again yelled at me, and he began to show me kindness whenever he could. A few days later when we moved to Sambok Moan, he was appointed as the commandant, and I was his friend.

Notes

1. Haing Ngor, *Survival in the Killing Fields* (New York: Carroll & Graf, 1987), 145.

2. "Forced Marriage and the Khmer Rouge," IntLawGrrls, October 7, 2010. http://intlawgrrls.blogspot.com/2010/10/forced-marriage-and-khmer-rouge.html.

3. Ngor, 213.

Chapter Seven

IN THE PRESENCE
OF MY ENEMIES

A Table Prepared

You serve me a six-course dinner
right in front of my enemies.

—Psalm 23:5 THE MESSAGE

To be slowly starved to death in a roomful of similarly
suffering victims seems to me to be a much more
excruciating and horrible way to die than simply being
marched off to a mass grave pit and smashed
on the back of the head with an iron bar.[1]

—Craig Etcheson

IT **SOUNDS** obvious, but there were no pens or books at Sambok Moan. But there were plenty of hoes and shovels and baskets. Among the prisoners were former members of parliament, professionals, police officers, and military officers. I was the youngest prisoner—and the only Christian.

Soon the other prisoners came up with a name for me. I was "Calendar Man" because every day I kept track of the date. That's how I know I spent exactly one year, three months, and thirteen days in prison, most of them at Sambok Moan. Four hundred, seventy days. I also kept count of the number of bodies I buried there, more than a hundred. To me those months became a blur of illness, hunger, and fear, just as they were for the men whose bamboo beds were linked to mine at night. Even so, every morning as I prayed and remembered Scripture, I mentally recorded the date, and I knew I was anchored, not only in time and space but also in the God who created that day.

When I left Thavy and her family for prison, I had one shirt, one pair of pants, and my *kramar*. I had already patched my clothing with jute rice bags, which kept me decent but also uncomfortable because jute itches terribly. My long pants had become shorts.

I spent one-third of the sixteen months in Force Number Three, but I continued to work whenever I could so I could get Force Number One rations. But these rations, even for the strongest of us, were never enough.

Hunger gnawed at my stomach continually. Every morning I recited Psalm 23, "I shall not want" and "He prepares a table for me in the presence of my enemies," but it became harder and harder to believe.

Each morning the *cadres* called roll, and every evening, usually after we had a chance to bathe, without soap, in the stream that flowed between the prison and the fields, the officers would call roll again. Both times we would form a line and await inspection. The officer of the day was always a different man, to keep us watchful and afraid. We never had the benefit of a set routine.

One evening, at the end of a particularly long, hard day of work, I reached a state of near hysteria as I bathed in the stream. "Lord! I am so hungry," I cried.

I continued to pray as I removed my tattered shirt and pants and rubbed them between my hands in the water. It was springtime, and the water was clear and fresh. There were some aquatic plants on the banks of the stream, and I hung my clothes on them for the remaining moments before the prison whistle would summon us back to camp. Other prisoners were stooping to catch small crabs or fish in the shallow water near the bank. They put whatever they caught in their pockets. I had discovered these tiny morsels to be very unsatisfying, never enough to relieve my hunger. Besides, I had just about given up.

The whistle blew and I reached for my clothes: first

my pants, then my shirt. I held out my shirt to put it on, and it moved! I turned it inside out and discovered a huge prawn, more like a lobster, enough to feed eight people. I could already taste it. I was elated . . . until I remembered the inspection at roll call. How many times had I seen my fellow prisoners beaten for a small crab found in a pocket? Finding a prawn that size was a miracle. Getting it through the *cadres* would take another. I breathed a prayer for a second miracle.

I placed the prawn—that night's dinner, I dearly hoped—in my *kramar* and wrapped it around my head. I joined the queue and tried to look innocent. The soldiers patted my pockets but didn't even look at my scarf.

After that, almost every day at the same time, I placed my clothes on the plants that bent their branches into the water, and almost every day I caught a fish or a prawn. Our scarves came in handy for another reason as well. That night I gave the prawn to my friend Sai, who had been appointed our chef because he wasn't well enough to work. He cooked it to perfection, and then several of us had a prawn party. To avoid suspicion and to keep the aroma from wafting through the room where all three hundred prisoners slept, we held our *kramars* over our faces while we ate. This became an almost nightly routine.

Our diet often indicated just how desperate we were. And how creative. We produced a kind of beef jerky from ropes that were merely long strips of cured ox hide. One prisoner risked his life stealing one. He then beat the "rope," cut it into small strips, and shared them with us. We could chew on those rope pieces for hours.

I sensed the Holy Spirit telling me to walk around the rice bed one more time. Then a fish jumped out of a small pool right at my feet.

Sambok Moan was in an open field in the jungle, not in an established village, so there were no cultured plants for us to harvest and eat. Everything potentially edible was wild. Most of us did not know which plants were poisonous. In our hunger we made the risky assumption that cooking a plant might render it safe to eat. As far as I know, this totally uneducated guess worked every time. More than once, I was tempted to call the yellow plant we named "banana" (though it clearly wasn't) another name: manna. On a few occasions a prisoner found a dead puppy, hid it in his *kramar* or pocket, and delivered it to Chef Sai. Most of us had never experienced this "delicacy." On those evenings we asked, "What is this?"

"Don't ask," the chef said, "just eat."

Every morning the guards allowed us to use the latrines,

which were holes dug in the ground under a shelter of palm leaves, only if we saluted the Khmer Rouge and asked their permission. Just before daybreak one morning, I saluted the guard and walked to the facilities. On the way I passed a dry rice bed. As I walked by, I heard something moving and discovered a fish the size of my arm. I sensed the Holy Spirit telling me to walk around the bed one more time. When I did, a fish literally jumped out of a small pool right at my feet. I took the two fish back to the camp, and the chef prepared a feast. The words of Psalm 23, the only full chapter I knew, had become prophetic.

On the way to Sambok Moan, I was part of a group of eighteen prisoners. But that number swelled to three hundred men who now slept in one big structure made of bamboo and covered with a palm leaf roof. The guards watched us more closely, and roll call became very serious business. Prisoners who were caught trying to escape were summarily executed.

But our greatest enemies were malnutrition and disease. Much of this was due to the lack of sodium in our diets. Every day the cooks added a small amount of salt, about the size of a condensed milk can, to a pot of rice for three hundred prisoners. No wonder we all got sick. The primary ingredient in our bowls wasn't even rice, it was water. Even the water posed a problem. Only three prisoners at Sambok Moan were strong enough to carry the water containers, balanced on either side of a beam carried on the shoulders, from the stream to the camp. I was not one of those three.

The lives and deaths of prisoners at the larger, more notorious prison near Phnom Penh, Tuol Sleng, were documented more systematically than at Sambok Moan. Today rows of black-and-white portraits line the walls of a memorial there. I have seen them many times. It is like viewing, image after image, a brotherhood of suffering. In those faces I see so many similarities to my brothers at Sambok Moan: the sunken cheeks of the famished, the fearful, haunted eyes, the bandages over wounds, and the unmistakable marks of disease.

As I slept one night the Lord spoke to me in a dream: "You won't die. You will survive for My purpose."

Not only did the Lord assure me that I would not die, He also told me that only seven of my friends would survive. I wasn't sure why God would choose me when so many others did not survive; but the message was clear, and I believed it.

The next morning when I woke up, my limbs were numb. I couldn't move. I thought it was the end. I did not join the queue for roll call that morning—my first time to miss one day of work. Chef Sai reported my condition to the *cadres* at roll call. The senior *cadre* appointed me to make herbal tea for everyone instead of working in the fields. That way I could still get a food ration. Barely able to walk, I went to the makeshift kitchen and boiled water in three large pots. Several other prisoners were trying to grill small fish and crabs on the fire under the pots. The pots collided, and the water splashed on the fire. Steam blasted my face and arms and legs. The intense heat assaulted the skin beneath my flimsy clothing. I couldn't open my eyes. My body felt as if it was on fire. Though I knew God's plans for me, I cried out, "Oh Lord, take me home. I can't take it anymore!"

The senior *cadre* heard my cries. He found a prisoner who was a former medical doctor. The prisoner told me to improvise by treating my burns with fish sauce or toothpaste—two items we did not have. The closest thing we had was salt. The doctor put some in his mouth, then spit the mixture of salt and saliva on my wounds. I began to have violent muscle spasms, but I did not cry. The next morning the doctor combined *lapov* (pumpkin) leaves with water buffalo dung and created a paste that he put on my face. It was itchy and dried into a tight mask. When I washed it off, I could already tell it worked; I was healing. Today, I have no evidence of the burn anywhere on my body. To heal me God used a doctor who was willing to further improvise his improvisation.

Like the rest of the prisoners, I battled various infectious diseases. Sanitation was nonexistent, and everyone was as skinny and malnourished as the thin cows in Pharaoh's dream. Once when I had a bout with malaria, an herbalist in the camp treated me using an ancient traditional therapy. Using a broken bottle, he sliced open a bamboo stalk, rolled it into a ball, and allowed the ball to dry. These balls were placed on my skin and burned with charcoal. Traditional healers used this method for almost every ailment. Supposedly the burning deadens the affected nerves, thus eliminating the pain.

When I had a stomachache and my belly was swollen, this same healer burned six holes, three on either side of my navel. When I had a toothache, he burned two scars on both sides of my jaw. My wisdom tooth broke, and I had no feeling at all, so I guess there was some benefit to this kind of "medicine." Later when I suffered malaria, chef Sai, my closest friend in the prison, shared six of his twelve quinine tablets with me. The required dose was seven tablets, but I discovered God did not need that final tablet to heal me.

When I developed an eye infection that wouldn't heal and became almost too painful to bear, neither the healer nor the doctor could do anything. My eyes became inflamed and swollen. My near-blindness became public knowledge after I fell off one of the low wooden bridges in the rice fields because I couldn't see the ground at my feet. A Khmer Rouge nurse sprayed a cloudy, white liquid from a pop bottle into my eyes with a syringe, but my eyes got worse.

Again I was sent to work in the kitchen. My older half

sister Sovannary had been a cooking teacher and, thankfully, had taught me some basic cooking skills. But I had no opportunity to be creative; every day I just made pots of rice for all of my fellow prisoners. I still could not see well, and I was in continual pain. A *cadre* took pity on me and ushered me to a pot of simmering water, opened the lid, and made me lean over it with my eyes wide-open. "Bear it," he said, "it will heal you." Steam was something I knew about, and I had no desire to become acquainted with it again. But the *cadre* insisted, and I knew if I resisted or if I cried in pain, I would be punished. Surprisingly, the steam gave me some immediate relief, and the infection eventually healed.

Questions

There were two types of interrogation at Sambok Moan. First, there was the expected, routine kind. Twice every week we were taken from roll call to a clearing where we were asked at least a hundred questions. The questions were usually the same, but the interrogators varied.

Then there were the late-night surprise interrogations. We would be selected at random and awakened by a *cadre* who would march us deep into the forest for these "self-assessment sessions." Many of our fellow prisoners never returned from these.

A pattern developed early on. If you were plucked

from your cot early in the evening, you might just make it back before morning. If the moon was high or already beginning its descent, you were most likely walking to your death. A friend at Sambok Moan, a former pilot, had relatives in the Khmer Rouge who had fallen out of favor with the regime. When he revealed his identity to the *cadres*, he was marched into the jungle, interrogated, and severely beaten. When he returned, he told me, "No relative can help us now. All loyalty is to the *Angkar* alone. They are the center of our lives now."

I decided I would tell the truth
whenever I was questioned.
I had nothing to lose
and everything to gain.

These words echoed the Khmer Rouge teachings we heard every day. Pol Pot's Catholic school background seeped through the verbiage: "Love the *Angkar* with all your heart and with all your mind" or "The revolutionary leader must serve the people." Haing Ngor, who survived his captivity in another prison like mine, commented on how convincing the Khmer Rouge propaganda could be:

I found myself believing, for at least moments at a time, that the Khmer Rouge had done it. They had succeeded in remaking the country to their bold plans. They had erased the individual, except as a unit in a group. They had given us a new religion to devote ourselves to, and that religion was Angka. But when I looked more closely, the illusion fell apart. The people working in the canal were tired and malnourished and their clothes were torn. Just like me . . . The Khmer Rouge pushed their own beliefs to extremes, and in doing so turned them into lies.[2]

The *Angkar* held us all fast in this prison of lies. Their laws were an inescapable trap: "Thou shalt observe the rules of the people when speaking, sleeping, walking, standing, or seated, in amusement or in laughter." I wasn't sure how we could keep the rules in our sleep, but that's how pervasive the grip of *Angkar*'s control was on every one of us. Even in our dreams, we couldn't escape it.

Or could we? I remembered the words of Jesus in Luke 9:24: "For if you want to save your own life, you will lose it, but if you lose your life for my sake, you will save it" (GNT). I was ready to die. In death I would be untouchable. Death could spring me from the *Angkar*'s trap. The torture would be over. And so I decided I would tell the truth whenever I was questioned. I had nothing to lose and everything to gain.

Word got around that I could read and write and—an even more dangerous skill—I could also speak English. Many of the *cadres* were illiterate. Intimidated by the educated prisoners, they hated those of us who could read and write. But Mit Yem, the camp commandant, was not like his underlings. He invited me to teach him and a friend to read and write.

These lessons took place in the evening after the full day of labor. Mit Yem worked under Comrade So Phim, the Secretary of the Eastern Zone Communist Party, a group that ultimately opposed Pol Pot. His friend often rode past us on his bicycle as we worked, and from time to time he stopped to give me a small gift in gratitude for our lessons. As a result, some of the other prisoners thought I was a spy and avoided me. But I believe my relationship with him served to protect me from greater danger.

The prisoner count dwindled from 300 to 127. Of my friends only seven were left, the exact number the Lord had told me would survive. I began to expect my release. One dark night at midnight, a *cadre* entered our hut and called my name. I awakened my friend, the chef, and whispered to him some final instructions. I asked him to find my home village when he was released and inform my family that I had died. I made him repeat the name of my village and my family members several times until I was satisfied that he had memorized them. I gave him my pants and my shirt and tied my *kramar* around my waist. At that moment I assumed the survival God had promised in my dream meant an escape from prison directly to heaven.

Mit Yem himself led me into the rain forest. He told me the *Angkar Loeu*—the upper organization—wanted to see me. The farther we walked, the more I assumed I was to be executed. No one would hear my screams from there.

When we reached a clearing, he asked me to stand in front of ten military *cadres*. I recognized them as the top military officers of the Eastern Zone because they were all dressed in new black polyester uniforms, and all had several pens in their shirt pockets. In those days low-ranking military officers and soldiers wore black, rough cotton uniforms. Synthetic fabric was reserved for the uniforms of the elite.

"Do you speak English?"

I remembered a friend who was overheard uttering one French word, *compte*, which means "account." The spy who heard this word mistranslated it, thinking he said *contre*, which means "against." It was bad enough that my friend spoke in a foreign, imperialistic language, but he allegedly used that language to pronounce a counterrevolutionary word. He was beaten and left for dead. Speaking English was worse than speaking French. I would surely suffer the same fate as my friend.

"Yes, I do."

I waited for the words I knew would be next: "Take him away." But the commandant asked me another question:

"How good is your English?"

"About 60 percent," I estimated. I had not heard, spoken, or read English for almost two years.

"Okay," the commandant said.

He paused and turned on a radio. "That is good enough," he said, looking at the other *cadres* as if to get their approval.

The other men nodded and the commandant looked at me. "Would you please translate this program for us?"

Sambok Moan is near the Vietnam border, and it was possible to get a signal for BBC World. I translated a news broadcast and waited to hear what they would do with me.

The officer had one more question: "Are you a Christian?"

"Yes, I am."

They now had more than enough information to justify killing me. I had served their purpose. I still expected to be executed, now that they had used my translating skills for their purposes. The commandant motioned for a *cadre* to take me and ordered, "Take good care of him."

My knees were shaking. I had heard, "Take him away" enough times to know it meant, "Kill him." It only made sense that "Take good care of him" meant "Kill him and bury his body where no one can find it."

The *cadre* took me to another man and ordered food for me. It was the best meal I had eaten since leaving Phnom Penh. For the first time since the first days after my arrest, I ate enough to feel satisfied. Though I knew it was my last supper, a trick to make me lower my guard before the *cadre* dealt a killing blow to the back of my head, I savored every bite. When I finished the last morsel, the commandant ordered the *cadre* who had fed me, "From now on, take better care of him."

Mit Yem marched me back to the camp. The closer we got to my hut, the more clearly it dawned on me that my life had been spared. Then I mentally recited the words of Psalm 23: "You prepare a table before me in the presence of my enemies"—with a smile, relishing the words like a choice morsel of the finest food.

Just before we left the clearing, the *cadre* had given me some tobacco. I did not smoke, but many prisoners did, and to them tobacco was like gold. Many prisoners used tobacco as bargaining chips for rations. I toyed with bartering this precious stash for food. But I was so relieved, I gave it away and watched my friends have a tobacco party that for them was as much a celebration as our prawn party had been. But the real celebration came just a few days later.

I was released. All 126 of my fellow prisoners were

released as well. Most of the Eastern Zone's top officials no longer supported Pol Pot or the atrocities he committed. Chan Chakrey, one of their colleagues, had been arrested and charged with treachery. The Eastern Zone officials saw the writing on the wall; they would most likely be next. They planned to flee to Vietnam, and there was no way to keep the prison up and running without them. Besides, production was at a virtual standstill because we prisoners had become too weak to work.

Eventually So Phim, secretary of the Eastern Zone, was assassinated by Pol Pot. Cambodia's ordeal wasn't over. In fact, the killings were only escalating. But I could not deny the truth that God had anointed my head with oil, and my cup was overflowing with the knowledge of His goodness.

Notes

1. Craig Etcheson, "'The Number'—Quantifying Crimes against Humanity in Cambodia," 06/10/2008. www.mekong.net/cambodia/toll.htm.

2. Haing Ngor, *Survival in the Killing Fields* (New York: Carroll & Graf, 1987), 215.

Chapter Eight

THE INTERSECTION
OF TWO WORLDS

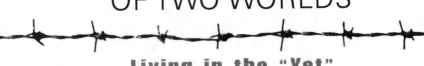

Living in the "Yet"

Our strength lies in our intensive
attacks and our barbarity . . . After all, who
today remembers the genocide of the Armenians?

—Adolf Hitler

Nothing fixes a thing so intensely
in the memory as the wish to forget it.

—Michel de Montaigne

In my alarm I said, "I am cut off from
your sight!" Yet you heard my cry
for mercy when I called to you for help."

—Psalm 31:22 NIV

SOMETIMES numbers tell a story better than words. Sometimes words just aren't enough. The arithmetic of torture and murder can thrive, undetected, beneath a cloak of rhetoric. Pol Pot was a master of deceptive oratory. He labeled the Khmer Rouge's enemies "microbes," echoing the Nazis' manner of referring to human beings as soulless objects, using the word *Konserve*, "canned goods," to refer to prisoners in their concentration camps. Pol Pot and his inner circle declared that anyone suspected of treachery must be "exterminated," "swept aside," or "smashed." This directive becomes even more disturbing when you do the math associated with the *Angkar*'s systematic annihilation of the people they labeled nothing more than a microscopic disease.

Between the years 1975 and 1979, some 158 prisons dotted the Cambodian landscape. There were 309 mass grave sites with an estimated total of 19,000 grave pits.[1] In September 1977 Pol Pot visited China. In October, not long after his return, 418 prisoners in Tuol Sleng were executed on a single day. Prison records document on "other days that month . . . the execution of 179 prisoners, 88 prisoners, and 148 prisoners respectively."[2]

But the documents left behind at Tuol Sleng offer only half of the history of those years. A collection of papers kept by the Khmer Rouge secret police, the *Santebal*, tells the rest. Discovered in 1996, this hefty archive includes seemingly endless records of confessions, the final breaths of tortured prisoners. The word *Santebal* means "keeper of the peace." Instead they kept written proof that they destroyed peace.

These records also reveal the growing paranoia among the elite knot of leaders with Pol Pot at its center. Despite the Khmer Rouge mantra of inclusion and equality, this group was small and exclusive. The conversations recorded by the *Santebal* have a distinctly "Big Brother" flavor. Chan Chakrey, commander of the Eastern Zone division, was, according to Pol Pot, someone to watch because of his supposed connection to Vietnam: "We must pay attention to what he says, to see [whether] he is a traitor who will deprive himself of any future." Chakrey's deputy was also a person of interest to Pot: "We must be totally silent . . . we must watch their activities." Chakrey was later sent to Tuol Sleng prison. His successor, the author of these accounts, was himself arrested not much later.[3]

Everyone in my country, from the very top to the very bottom, was the same. We existed on the edge of a thousand grave pits. Each of us was like Chan Chakrey, a man who could unwittingly "deprive himself of any future."

My Fixed Point

Autobiographers have certain rights. Foremost is the right to tell the truth from his own point of view. But inherent in this right is the responsibility to tell it as accurately as possible. That is why I have occasionally stepped away from my own story to give you a wider view of the events between 1975 and 1979. My story isn't mine alone. It also belongs to my fellow Cambodians. It belongs to the 1.7 million who died and all the others, like me, who survived. You cannot fully understand my story unless you grasp at least part of theirs. We shared the same context.

Yes, I suffered.

Yet I shouted praise in my heart.

Yes, I was afraid.

Yet I learned to trust my Lord.

Yes, so much was taken away.

Yet so much was given.

But context, for the believer, has another dimension. Christians stand with one foot in this world and one foot in another. And that other world is our real home. Sometimes the contrast between these two worlds is especially jarring. This world is full of hate and revenge and insecurity. That other world is full of love and redemption and stability. This world hurts us. That world saves us. This world makes no sense. That world gives us perspective. But one is no less real than the other.

My story, like yours if you are a Christ-follower, took

place at the intersection of these two worlds. Therein lies my dilemma. There is no way to tell you about the Killing Fields without revealing the raw horror of this world at its worst. And there is also no way to be honest about those years without including the blessings and joy of that other world. God brought His best gifts to bear in the worst situations. I do not want to present either truth lightly. Yes, I suffered. Yet I shouted praise in my heart. Yes, I was confused and disheartened by what I saw. Yet I heard the voice of the Holy Spirit leading me too many times to count. Yes, I was afraid. Yet I learned to trust my Lord. Yes, so much was taken away. Yet so much was given.

"Yet" is the geographical fixed point for the follower of Christ. It acknowledges the darkness while simultaneously turning our attention to the light. It shifts all glory away from suffering and to the God who meets us in that suffering. "Yet" is a miracle word that we utter by God's grace alone. It is a pivot point, a tiny word that connects the worst experience with the truth of God's redeeming love and power. My life isn't the only one that has a resounding "yet" at its center. You'll find *yet* over and over in the Psalms:

> Why are you downcast, O my soul? Why so disturbed within me? Put your hope in God, for I will *yet* praise him, my Savior and my God. (Psalm 42:5–6 NIV, emphasis added)

When our fathers were in Egypt, they gave no thought to your miracles; they did not remember your many kindnesses, and they rebelled by the sea, the Red Sea. *Yet* he saved them for his name's sake, to make his mighty power known. (Psalm 106:7–8 NIV)

My God, my God, why have you forsaken me? Why are you so far from saving me, so far from the words of my groaning? O my God, I cry out by day, but you do not answer, by night, and am not silent. *Yet* you are enthroned as the Holy One; you are the praise of Israel. (Psalm 22:1–3 NIV)

If you read a psalm with this dramatic word, you may notice there are times when the "yet" doesn't come until the very end, sometimes the last verse. The psalmist is so discouraged, so terrified, and so beaten down, it takes the balance of the psalm for him to get to that all important "yet." But he does get there. And so did I. Not always immediately but eventually.

In the Meantime

"Where is my husband?"

The first familiar face I saw when I was released to the village of Phom Po, just fourteen kilometers from Sambok Moan, was the beautiful wife of my friend Mr. Vorn. Her husband had been a large, jovial man before the months we spent together in prison. He died small enough for me to carry his body over my left shoulder. Like so many prisoners whose smoking habits led them to barter food for tobacco, I watched my friend waste away until he was not much more than skin and bones. I remembered Mr. Vorn in life, but I couldn't forget his death. Or his burial. His was the body I could not fully cremate because of the rain. When his wife approached me, all I could think of were his charred remains and my desperation as I struggled to bury him.

I could not bear to tell her. Besides, on my way to Phom Po, the village head had taken me to visit the area commune leader. He said, "Do not tell what you have seen." It was both a warning and a threat. I had spent over a year becoming a mute *kapok* tree, and I wasn't about to change now. I looked at my friend's wife, remembering when Mr. Vorn was alive and well, and said, "The last time I saw him . . ." I did not say, "The last time I saw him *alive* . . ." but that's what I meant.

She left me with a tiny flicker of hope in her eyes. I knew it was a false hope, but it was something. To survive, we all needed hope.

Soon after I was released, the malaria I had contracted in Sambok Moan returned with a vengeance. Though she was in her seventies, my dear friend Chhae took me in. For many days I remained in a deep coma while Chhae tenderly ministered to me. In my dreams, I saw my real mother and she hugged me. I cried and called out to her, but my mother wasn't there. The hands that fed me and the arms that held me were Mae Chhae's. During this time, she became my second mother. We remained close until her death in 2010 at the age of 108. The Khmer Rouge had seized a coconut grove that had been in her family for years, leaving her only five trees. Mae Chhae fed me coconut juice from those trees. She bartered her dogs for quinine tablets. She also administered traditional healing methods to my broken body. She saved my life.

For a brief time, Thavy and I were reunited, but never for more than a few months. In Phom Po we shared a one-room house with other members of her father's family. Our first child, a son named Lyda, was born a year after I was released from prison. Although we had a child, the village authorities questioned the legitimacy of our marriage. Their questions and the constant hovering of the young *chhlop*, Khmer Rouge spies, added to the fragility of our already unstable relationship.

They not only killed individual traitors, they also killed everyone who had served under that person.

We were never physically well during this time. Lack of food made us vulnerable to the diseases that circulated in the villages. Thavy developed the same skin condition I had contracted in prison. This disease, probably a combination of ringworm and other infectious illnesses, was thought to be incurable. It only added to our sense of hopelessness.

When I was released from Sambok Moan, the village leader of Phom Po came to fetch me. The commandant, Mit Yem, left a letter for him. In this letter, he pleaded with the leader to "take care of" me. This time I understood there was no hidden meaning in the phrase. For a short while, Thavy and I were given preferential treatment, then the village leader was arrested. As the *Angkar* began to purge the country of their enemies with more and more intensity, they not only killed individual traitors, they also killed everyone who had served under that person—along with all their family members. Our protection in the village was short-lived.

Protection was something Thavy craved. Soon after we were reunited, we were again forced to relocate. Our son, Lyda, who continually suffered from dysentery, died in a later relocation. Then Thavy became pregnant with twins. Children and pregnant women were the most vulnerable, so she was doubly at risk. Just before the twins were due, in April 1979, while we were walking toward Phnom Penh, hoping to escape the Killing Fields of Pursat, we met Thavy's father, her three motherless brothers, and her aunt.

It was clear to me that Thavy wanted to leave me and join them. Yet she pleaded with me to stay with her until she gave birth to the twins. I was present for the birth of our daughters, Sisera and Thama. We came back to Kampong Phnom Village—where our romance began and where I decided to become Thavy's common-law husband. As soon as she was able, Thavy again began to talk of leaving. Instead of continuing on the migration with me as my wife, Thavy chose to follow her father. She was determined, she said in no uncertain terms, to live with her father for the rest of her life. Thus our relationship ended a few months after the end of the genocide. Thankfully all of her family survived, including our daughters.

The Long March to More Captivity

Early in 1978, Cambodia's first war with Vietnam began. Pol Pot's grip on the country was falling apart, and he couldn't help but know it. His response was predictable.

I have alluded to the continual relocating of buildings that took place all over the countryside. Perhaps this dismantling of a structure, only to move it a short distance and rebuild it exactly as it was before, was nothing more than busywork for prisoners who needed an extra dose of hard labor. But the symbolism was just too transparent to miss.

From 1975 until 1979, beginning with the evacuation of Phnom Penh, my fellow citizens and I participated in one exodus after another, sometimes covering a few kilometers and sometimes traversing the entire width of the country. We were continually on the move, but this time there was a reason for it.

Vietnam had always been a threat, but in 1978 it intensified. So we fled the provinces closest to Vietnam, the Eastern Zone, and moved toward the northwest and a friendlier neighbor, Thailand. In every possible way we were "encouraged" to head west. While still in Phom Po, however, planes flew overhead and dropped tracts, ostensibly from the Viet Cong, claiming they had won the war and we could all return home. By then we were skeptical of everything, so there was no mad dash to our villages. We later found out Pol Pot's pilots flew those planes and dropped the bogus messages. The *Angkar* wasn't slowing down. They were racing to eradicate as many of their enemies as they could—until Vietnam put a stop to their madness.

In Phom Po, the village *cadres* were removed and replaced with younger ones. We all understood that this new, grassroots leadership was even more dangerous for us, so we decided to leave for Subzone 24, not far away. We had not been arrested, but our decision was clear.

God's Favor

Most days during these three months, I felt distressed enough to say, "Oh God, why did You bring me here?" *And yet . . .*

God's favor, which was always present, broke through the darkness in visible ways. I had survived four years of darkness—darkness punctuated by brief bursts of almost blinding light. Four years covered by a blanket of suffering that was pierced through with hope. That is why I could look around and still say the word *yet*.

Sometimes God used a provision—a bag of rice laid at my feet like a gift, a prawn caught in my shirt, six quinine tablets—to enable me to say *yet* and thereby hope again in Him. Often He used His Word—Psalm 23 and snatches of other verses I remembered. Hymns, dreams, prayer vigils, these things encouraged me. But many times, from April 1975 until February 1979, God used *people* to send me the personal message that He loved me, He would protect me, and would provide for me. Chhawn, Song, chef Sai, Mit Yem, and Mae Chhae. As you read on, you'll see that people, while capable of unimaginable evil, are also God's most effective bearers of light.

Notes

1. Cambodian Genocide Program, Interactive Geographic Database. www.yale.edu/cgp/maplicity.html.

2. Ben Kiernan, "Notes from a Slaughterhouse," *Bangkok Post*, May 30, 1999. www.yale.edu/gsp/publications/slaughter.html.

3. "The Khmer Rouge National Army: Order of Battle," January 1976, Cambodian Genocide Program. www.yale.edu/cgp/army_v3.html.

Chapter Nine

THE
KILLING FIELDS

The Unspeakable Has a Name

Do good to your friends to
keep them, to your enemies to win them.

—Benjamin Franklin

I will not testify, including answer
any question put to me during trial . . .

—Ieng Sary, former deputy prime minister under Pol Pot

Awake, and rise to my defense!
Contend for me, my God and Lord.

—Psalm 35:23 NIV

IF YOU know anything about Cambodia's history, the years 1978 to 1979 are the ones you know the most about. The western fields, where so many died, are most likely the areas you might recognize on a map or in a photo: Battambang or Choeung Ek or the Chankiri Tree, where children of alleged traitors were hung by the ankles until they died.

And if you know anything about the men and women who put the word "killing" in the Killing Fields, you are familiar with the most notorious among them: Pol Pot, Nuon Chea, Ieng Sary, Son Sen, Ta Mok, and Kaing Guek Eav, also known as Comrade Duch, the commandant of Tuol Sleng who stood trial before an international tribunal in 2009 and pleaded guilty to personally overseeing the tortures and deaths of more than 15,000 prisoners.

It would be a mistake to hear the names of each *cadre* in my story, each *Mit Neary* (female *cadre*), each subzone head, and assume every one of these was as cunning as an Ieng Sary or as violent as a Comrade Duch. That is the common error of the novice historian. The real story is always much more complex.

Mit Suon (Comrade Suon), the man who arrested me when I arrived in Subzone 24, was nothing like these men. A few months after he arrested me, Mit Suon and I walked with a large group to Neak Leung, where I was to travel by boat to Phnom Penh. The night he arrested and interrogated me, I noticed his lighter hadn't worked. For some reason I had kept my ration of flints although I didn't smoke. I offered him one of my flints. It's amazing how a small gesture in desperate times can immediately cement a friendship.

The likelihood of survival
was lessening for all of us,
no matter our community.
Still, I asked God for a miracle.

By the time we arrived at the boat, he begged me to find a way not to go. He understood that the migration to the northwest was anything but safe. He gave me his *kramar*—tied it around my neck—and, weeping, he blessed me. I was not leaving out of any sense of duty to the *Angkar*. I was just hoping to find my family. Mit Soun was yet another reminder along the way of God's favor toward me.

Wooden cargo boats linked together—four paired boats in all—carried two hundred families on the Lower Mekong River to Phnom Penh. The boats were coated in resin and covered with a simple roof.

Pol Pot had given us a name. We were all *Puok Kbal Yuon Kluon Khmer*, or Pro-Vietnam Cambodians in the Eastern Zone. Right after I boarded, I discovered I had been appointed a leader of the entire group of more than six hundred. I wasn't sure what that would entail, but I recognized God at work on my behalf. I was also certain Mit Soun had arranged it.

The people were restless and afraid. Rumors circulated that the boats were to be sunk by the Khmer Rouge. Given the propensity of the *Angkar* to offer hope to a mass of people and then surprise them with a quick trip to a remote area and a shovel to the back of the head, this rumor wasn't far-fetched. When we reached the city, a *cadre* took me on a tour of the new Phnom Penh. It was hardly recognizable. Boeung Trabek High School had become a rice field, bowing to the Khmer Rouge motto, *Plant Land.* The literal translation of this phrase means to plant without leaving any span of land vacant, to cover the earth. Little by little, wherever they could, they were getting it done.

Bethany Church had been converted to a warehouse. Nothing was as I remembered it. Instead of going next to the station, where the six hundred boat passengers waited for a train, I was driven to Chbar Ampeou, the still-famous marketplace just across the Bassac River. There I worked all day gathering blankets, scarves, clothing (mainly jeans), and medicine for the people under my supervision. Men in black uniforms swarmed the marketplace.

I saw my first movie that night. I was so busy gathering supplies, I missed the train that left the station at

5:00. So I stayed to watch the film. Chbar Ampeou had an open-air theater where the Khmer Rouge showed propaganda reels. Healthy, happy farmworkers filled the screen, their hoes digging into the soil to the tune of rousing Khmer songs. I knew better than to believe the messages in the movie, but it provided a welcome diversion. After the movie, I spent the night waiting for the next train, which was scheduled to arrive in the morning.

I, along with my six hundred charges, boarded the train at 7:00 in the morning and arrived in Svay Don Keo at 5:00 that evening. Right after we disembarked, I went to the river to pray. I felt the weight of responsibility for so many lives. A woman with light skin approached me and asked, "Where are you from?"

I was tired and hungry and preoccupied. "Subzone 24."

"What village are you from?"

I told her my uncle's village instead of my own. I didn't mean to mislead her; I was just not thinking clearly. Because of my mistake, we discovered we had mutual friends and she decided she could trust me. She explained that everyone at Svay Don Keo, where our group had just arrived, was to be divided into four communities. Those in *Kang Roy 4*, Community Number Four, would have the best chance of survival. They would be given better supplies of food, almost plentiful in contrast with the other three groups. Cassava, coconut, and rice, not the watered-down kind we were used to.

Community Number Four sounded like the land of milk and honey. What I didn't know was that over the past few months, the killing had been escalating. The likelihood of survival was lessening for all of us, no matter our community. Still, I asked God for a miracle. I asked Him to help me transfer to Community Number Four, if I wasn't already assigned there.

The woman also warned me to watch out for any man who wore a black *Montagut* T-shirt. These French-made shirts were the uniform of *cadres* who could, like the men who wore pens in their pockets, kill at will. Finally, she pointed toward the west and said, "Those are the Killing Fields."

I had never heard those words. It was hard to imagine fields more red with blood than where I had already been.

Yet there were moments
when God's favor
dazzled like a lone star
in a pitch-black sky.

I returned to the station, where I used some of my rations to barter for a grilled rooster. As I was eating it and enjoying a moment of relative peace, I heard someone say, "Is anyone here named Vann? The Vann who just arrived today from the Eastern Zone?"

I looked up and saw a *cadre* in a *Montagut* T-shirt approaching me. He pointed to me and said, "Come here. The *Angkar* is waiting for you."

The officer asked if I could look over the list of names from my boat and their designations to each of the four communities. He said the list wasn't divided equally, and he didn't have time to change it. Could I suggest a different way to organize the people? If he knew the lethal difference among the four groups, his manner didn't indicate it. The list he handed me offered no clue either.

If I had not met the woman at the river, I would never have known that the lists for the first three communities were essentially death sentences. The first page began with the names assigned to Community Number One, and I drew in a breath as I noticed my name in the first column. For the rest of the night, I shuffled names until I had moved as many people as I possibly could, including myself, to Community Number Four. God's favor wasn't for me alone. Whenever I could, His favor was something I must share with others.

Pinpoints of Light

I lived in Svay Don Keo in Pursat Province from October 1978 until two months after Vietnam seized Phnom

Penh in January 1979. This period still held a miasma of beatings and more dead bodies than I could count. Yet there were moments when God's favor dazzled like a lone star in a pitch-black sky. These are the moments I choose to recall.

Because I was the leader of the boat people who traveled from Neak Loeung, I was the go-to person for the *cadres* who guarded us. But that didn't guarantee my safety. Upon my arrival at the prison camp, I was asked to establish and run a community kitchen. The food for our group was not as plentiful as the woman at the river predicted, but it was far better than the other three communities. Then, from October to February, our supplies dwindled as sharply as the body count rose. On my second day a woman was sent from a nearby village to help me. She later told me she was a *Khmer Cham*, an Islamic spy, chosen by the camp leaders to watch me.

Hunger and illness were still our constant companions, but what caused us to despair was the continual killing. The *Angkar* was increasingly less covert and more reckless in their attempts to snuff out any life they deemed a threat. And almost everyone was guilty of *something*. At any time and in every place in the camp, prisoners would be selected, trussed up like cattle, and dragged away to be murdered. The tricks the *cadres* used to lure unsuspecting prisoners to their deaths became more and more transparent. I was moved from the *Kang Roy 4* to a mobile unit, a *Kang Chalat*, where I shared a hut with three men, Thorl, Chan, and Rain. Of the three, Chan and Rain were killed, their bodies disposed of in the bush nearby.

This was also when so many of the forced weddings took place, followed the next day by mass slaughter. Entire groups would be told what at first were convincing lies: *Go to the next Kang Roy to collect salt and rice to store in warehouses; Gather with other families to start a new community; Move here or there because your skills are needed elsewhere.* These tricks were effective . . . and fatal. There was no escaping the presence of death; its sound and smell permeated everything.

Soon after I arrived, a guard whispered to me that the commandant, a *Khmer Cham*, or Muslim, named Yoeun, was to be replaced. Apparently he had been caught in adultery. The Khmer Rouge had strict morals about loyalty in marriage. This commandant, the guard confided, would be leaving a list of tasks to be done. One of those tasks was eliminating all 150 members of our *Kang Roy*, including me. I could only hope the man who replaced him would not inherit the same duty.

One day, though I was continually hungry, I decided to fast. I went to the threshing floor during the lunch period (there were two daily meals: lunch and dinner) to pray. I felt I was truly in the valley of the shadow of death. I cried out, "Oh Lord, of my three friends who had shared the hut with me here, two have been killed by the Khmer

Rouge. Have You brought me here to die like them?"

As I prayed, a short, curly haired man I had never seen approached and called out, "Hey Charles de Gaulle, time for lunch."

I assumed he called me that because I was taller than he was, but I didn't think it was funny. In Cambodian culture, if a man speaks to you with both hands in the pockets of his pants, it is a gesture of disdain. But if a man puts his hands in the pockets of his shirt, it is just the opposite. This man's hands were thrust in his shirt pockets. So I felt I could be honest with him. "I am fasting," I said, "because to go with lunch or to go without it, I will still die. Two of my friends who shared my hut were just killed. Sooner or later I will be trapped and killed too."

"If you want to die, don't eat. You'll die of starvation before anyone has a chance to kill you," the man said. "But if you don't want to die, eat."

I was stricken by his soft-spoken manner. I felt ashamed for telling my sorrows to a complete stranger, so I followed him to the camp and ate. That afternoon, while there was still plenty of daylight for work, the bell that normally summoned us from the fields at 6:00 rang at 4:00. Everyone assembled quickly, all of us fearing the worst.

We were informed by one of the officers that the commandant had been removed and a new leader would be taking his place immediately. The short, curly haired man who had met me at the threshing floor stepped to the center of the clearing, and the guard introduced him as our new commandant. I began trembling. What if he remembered our conversation? What if he took offense at my boldness? Surely he had tricked me, and death would be the reward for unburdening myself to him. He cleared his throat and spoke to us gently. "You are all like water and I am like a fish. A fish can't survive without the water; neither can I without you. We must stay together and care for one another."

This man's straightforward manner and his obvious concern for our welfare disarmed my despair. He then sought me with his eyes and nodded with the hint of a smile. I wasn't sure if I was imagining it. Then he called out to me, and there was no mistake, "Come on, Charles de Gaulle," he said. "I will appoint you this very day my personal assistant."

I no longer felt the weight of a death sentence. I sensed that he could become not only a kind boss but also my good friend. And I was right. He continued to call me Charles de Gaulle and eventually asked me if I would teach him to read and write.

On Trial

Mit Soeun, the new commandant, was sent to our community to supervise our work on an irrigation system for the region's rice paddies. In Cambodia there are three harvests. First is the early harvest, just four months after the sowing season. This lasts just four months. The second harvest lasts five months, and the third, six months. I arrived at Svay Don Keo in the middle of the first harvest. In January, as the third harvest was drawing to a close, the entire community was mobilized to work on the system for watering the rice fields.

Although our people were dying daily, up to one hundred new people were added to the camp each day, as Pol Pot pushed the country westward out of Vietnam's grasp. Our task was to build as many *tomnup*—dams— as we could and dig as many *pralai*—canals—as possible. We were never idle. Though only married people or teenagers qualified for this "honor," everyone in Community Number Four was considered part of Workforce Number One—healthy, strong workers. After almost four years of hard labor, illness, continual fear, and often torture, those of us who were left in "force" were swiftly losing our ability to perform the jobs the *Angkar* pressed upon us.

During this time Mit Soeun relied on me heavily. As his deputy, I was his right-hand man. His trust in me defied the camp's power structure. I was not a "base" person, someone who had lived in the area since 1975, *and* I had come from the east, which was tantamount to associating with Vietnam. I was thankful for our friendship, but others found it suspicious, and found *me* suspicious. One in particular, a "base" man I'll call Mr. Sun, was threatened by the influence he felt I had but did not deserve. This man was friends with the secret police in our camp. He went to them and, as you say in the West, "ratted me out."

At that time there were three hundred men and women working in our *Kang Chalat*. Mr. Sun and his group of thugs called for a meeting with every person in the camp and with Mit Soeun. It was high drama, a trial staged late at night in order to frighten me and, they hoped, get me killed. I'm sure they all assumed theirs was an airtight case, which not even my friendship with the commandant could save me. They expected Mit Soeun to capitulate in their favor and drive the final nails in my coffin. I use the word figuratively because my corpse would have been simply thrown into the bush. In turn they accused me and Mit Soeun acted as my defense attorney:

Accusation Number One: The prisoner, Vann, made selfish decisions without getting proper approval from his superiors.

Mit Soeun: "Everyone here understands how stressful this time is for all of us. I cannot be here to make every decision about the digging of the canals or the building of the dams. I made it very clear to the accused that I trusted him to make certain decisions without me. Not once has he made a decision I would not have made myself, had I been present. Not once has he overstepped my instructions. You see, contrary to what you say, he did have the proper approval for everything he did."

Accusation Number Two: The prisoner showed preferential treatment to a young woman. (*Note:* The Khmer Rouge considered this tantamount to treason.)

Mit Soeun: "Allow me to call two *Mit Neary*, who serve as nurses, to testify on Vann's behalf. I believe you will then understand that the accused was acting in keeping with their specific instructions. The young woman in question suffers from an 'issue of blood' and has fainted on numerous occasions. She would be too weak to work unless allowed to remain in Group Number One, where she can receive the proper rations. Therefore the nurses insisted the accused give her a revised work schedule. Listen to their testimony. They will make it clear that the accused was only acting according to their orders."

Accusation Number Three: The prisoner knowingly slowed down the work by sabotaging the hoes and spades used to dig canals and build dams.

Mit Soeun: "As you all know, the grandfathers and grandmothers in our community weave our baskets and repair our farm implements. I will now call three grandpas to testify that not only did the accused, indeed, order them to cut bamboo from broken handles, but this 'sabotage,' as you call it, was a brilliant way to use worthless tools to fix the reparable ones. You have all seen how many workers are injured when the blades fly from the handles of our spades and hoes. The prisoner has corrected this problem by wedging the shims, sliced from old handles, into the gaps where the handle is threaded into the blade of newer tools."

With Mit Soeun's expert testimony on my behalf, there was nothing left but for Mr. Sun and the others to back down. But I enjoyed only a brief spell of relief. We began to receive orders to evacuate farther away, toward Thailand and "the mountain" where Pol Pot was supposedly gathering his forces and licking his wounds. Mit Soeun and I both knew these messages spelled doom for all of us, so we devised clever ways not only to delay our departure but also to move the people in the opposite direction whenever we could. Every time a messenger arrived with a warrant for our relocation, Mit Soeun was nowhere to be found. Instead I accepted the orders and said I would deliver them to him whenever he returned. But who knew when that would be?

If the *Angkar* could use propaganda to strike fear into our hearts, why couldn't we do the same to them? Mit Soeun and I became quite skillful at warning the local *cadres* that the Vietnamese were nearby. If we suspected Pol Pot's regime wanted us to go one direction, we made sure everyone thought that was exactly where a squad of Viet Cong were hiding out. It worked for a while. But then,

just as we were finding it impossible to avoid the direc-
tives from the *Angkar*, we were freed. Vietnam had seized
control of the entire country and we could—this time it
was true—go home. But before I describe the return journey to Phnom Penh, allow me to take you back once again
to the day the nightmare—for all of us—began.

Chapter Ten

MARTYRS, MENTORS,
AND MAINSTAYS

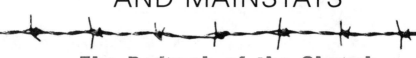

The Bedrock of the Church

The blood of the martyrs
is the seed of the church.

—Tertullian

And now, years after nearly being exterminated,
Christianity is growing in Cambodia,
despite the new government's clamp-down
on non-Buddhist religious activities.[1]

—Chuck Colson

Precious in the sight of the
Lord is the death of his saints.

—Psalm 116:15

THE NIGHT before the siege of Phnom Penh in 1975, the American embassy got word of the attack. I'm sure it was a harrowing experience for them, huddling behind blacked-out windows and waiting for the sound of friendly aircraft coming to pluck them out of our hell. Even as the choppers landed on the roof of the embassy, I'm sure those inside trembled with fear.

At the World Vision child care office near the Olympic stadium and the embassy, another kind of trembling occurred. Sixty of us met with my dear friends and fellow World Vision staffers, Chhirc Taing and Minh Thien Voan, to pray. These two men were relatives as well as brothers in Christ. Voan, the Cambodian director of World Vision, was personally responsible for my employment there. There was nothing routine about this prayer meeting. We trembled because we were keenly aware of the dangers surrounding us. And we trembled because we sensed the presence of God. Let me tell you how we came to be there on that historic evening.

Chhirc and I had just spent three packed days leading a seminar for sixty pastors and lay leaders at the Takhmau Bible School south of Phnom Penh. Some of Lon Nol's troops had taken refuge at the college, and on the last day of the seminar the Khmer Rouge attacked. We were caught in the cross fire. Mortar rounds fell around us like rain in the monsoon season. Because the fighting was escalating all the way from Takhmau to Phnom Penh, we weren't sure we could make the drive home safely. We were stuck.

Chhirc called Voan, who called the presidential office, only to be informed that Lon Nol had already been evacuated to Hawaii. Even so, Voan finally found a sympathetic ear, and we were given official permission to travel north to Phnom Penh. On our way back, we held our breath each time we passed a checkpoint. The trigger-happy soldiers recognized the World Vision van, and often they recognized me. I had made this trip many times and the authorities knew I was not a Communist or a spy.

We dropped off the other leaders at their homes, then Chhirc and I headed to the child care office. Like our American neighbors at their embassy, we knew something remarkable and possibly tragic was happening in Cambodia. Unlike them, we didn't know what it was.

We spent the entire night praying for ourselves, for our church, for the future of our nation, and for other nations. And we thanked God for rescuing us that very day. In the morning Chhirc kissed me good-bye and charged all of us with the message of Romans 13:1: "Let every person be subject to the governing authorities. For there is no authority except from God, and those that exist have been instituted by God." He reminded us to be as gentle as doves and as wise as snakes (Matthew 10:16). Then he and Voan left with their Bibles and some gospel tracts.

I never saw either man again.

My Own Book of Martyrs

"I never saw him again."

It is something we Cambodians say a lot when we recall those years. What Jesus said about blessings is also true about suffering: "He causes his sun to rise on the evil and the good, and sends rain on the righteous and the unrighteous" (Matthew 5:45 NIV). The Khmer Rouge meted out misery without prejudice. Christians weren't any less targeted than Buddhists, Muslims, or those who wore no religious label. And Christians weren't the only ones who bore it nobly. My Communist mentor, Mr. At Veth, and his friend Huy Nim both died in prison. Years later, I found At Veth's picture at Tuol Sleng. He opted to kill himself rather than accept the inevitable and allow the Khmer Rouge to kill him.

Those who died martyrs' deaths died as they lived.
During good times and bad, what sets Christians apart is *who they are.*

In 1975 there were twenty-seven evangelical churches in Phnom Penh and an estimated ten thousand believers.

In 1979 only two hundred Christians were left alive. Of the thirty-three pastors who served in the city, only six remained. The Catholic priests, nuns, and teachers were also targeted and either died or were deported.[2]

I cannot claim that the Christians were the only martyrs, nor were they the only martyrs who suffered like saints. But I have to ask, Were we different? And, if so, *how* were we different? The answers are not simple. We were scattered all over the countryside so we could observe only what took place right around us. After the events of April 1975, I did not speak with another Christian for several years. So I can tell only what I know. And what I know is the character of the men and women who died martyrs' deaths. They died as they lived. Perhaps that is their major distinction. During good times and bad, what sets Christians apart is *who they are.*

Brother Chhirc

When he was a young man, Chhirc Taing's parents sent him from Cambodia to a military academy in France. His parents were Christians who hid a Bible in their son's suitcase before he left home. Chhirc read that Bible over and over and as a result met Jesus Christ personally. He returned to Cambodia and served in the army, rising to the rank of major.

From the moment he prayed to receive Christ in his tiny dorm room in France, Chhirc was committed to advancing the gospel and never looking back. No matter the situation, he did not hide the fact that he was a believer. For five years, between 1965 and 1970, Cambodians were not allowed to worship freely. Chhirc worked tirelessly during this time to make a way for the church to meet openly. He and Voan met and shared an immediate connection. Soon after Voan became the director of World Vision, Chhirc joined him on staff.

Major Chhirc Taing was a force to be reckoned with. During my first years as a follower of Christ, he was the most influential person in my life. I heard about him before I met him. He had just returned from Scotland, and there was quite a buzz about his life and ministry in the Christian community. My curiosity piqued, I began to long for a personal relationship with this man. I knew I needed a mentor, and I decided even before I met Chhirc that he would be mine. That's what I prayed for.

Between services one Sunday, I stood at the entrance to Bethany Church. I attended both the Khmer and the English services, so I could improve my English. A car pulled up and a middle-aged, short man with a fair complexion and a wide, infectious smile jumped out and climbed the stairs toward me. "Hello!" he said as he shook my hand. "Have you accepted Christ?"

This man really gets right to the point, I thought. I said that, yes, I had.

"Brother, you will never be sorry!" He patted my

shoulder. "You have made the greatest decision you could ever make."

This encounter reminds me of the two men who met the resurrected Jesus on the road to Emmaus. When they figured out, after the fact, that they had just met Jesus, they said to each other, "Did not our hearts burn within us . . . ?" (Luke 24:32). That's how I felt when I met Chhirc, though I didn't know who he was until later. He shook my hand, and an indescribable warmth flowed into my being.

Chhirc and I became friends, and his life immediately began to impact mine. Ours was more than an ordinary friendship. He was my Elijah, and I was his Elisha. But his life didn't touch mine alone. He was God's instrument to bring revival to Cambodia during the two years before 1975. In 1973, just before he left Scotland for Phnom Penh, he spoke at the Keswick Convention and pleaded with the free Christian world to pray for our country.

The last message he preached in Cambodia was from 2 Kings 2:1–15. In this passage Elisha cried out to Elijah for a double portion of his spirit before Elijah was taken into heaven. This was a uniquely Cambodian message for our unique times. Most of the Americans had already left, so Chhirc's challenge was laser-focused on the Khmer people. He called us to rise up as an Elisha generation. Perhaps he knew that he, our Elijah, would not be here to see the fruit of his ministry.

Chhirc lived what he taught. He modeled traits that

later carried me through the hardest of times. His wife and daughter were far away in Scotland. In our culture, as well as in the Communist ideal, most natural emotions are kept private, even discouraged. But Chhirc never concealed that he loved his family and missed them terribly. His love for his wife and daughter were all the more intense because he seemed to know he might never see them again. Before he left Scotland in 1973, he shared with his friends and family that God had called him back to Cambodia to die as a martyr.

He was vulnerable and honest, yet I never heard him speak ill of another. He stressed this habit to me as well. If I spoke in a negative or harsh way, he was quick to rebuke me, but always as gently as possible. I was a very young believer, yet he entrusted me with leadership. He asked me to lead a Sunday school class at Bethany, to teach an English class, and even to translate for guest speakers at the annual conference of the Khmer Evangelical Church. He taught me about the gifts listed in Romans 12 and gave me all kinds of opportunities to use them.

I always sensed Chhirc's hope about life. He hoped in the promise that I could become a faithful minister of the gospel. He also hoped in the Lord for bigger things. In 1973 there were close to seven thousand orphans in Phnom Penh. He and Minh Thien Voan went with World Vision president Stan Mooneyham to visit a group of 123 boys who were housed inside a barbed-wire enclosure. Throughout their visit they heard nearby gunfire. The two men left with a desire to do something about the problem of homeless children, especially those with medical needs. Voan, Sonne Son, and Chhirc began plans for a pediatric hospital. On the day they signed a contract for the land, they led a doctor to give his life to Christ. The men believed this was a sign that the compassion of Christ would, indeed, result in a new hospital for Cambodia's children. Chhirc followed the progress of this project until the Khmer Rouge seized Phnom Penh and all visible signs of hope were erased.

Chhirc kissed me good-bye, and I never saw him again. What happened next took me years to piece together. I now know he was still alive on April 20, 1975, because on that date he posted a letter from the French embassy to his wife, Bophana:

Dear Bophana,

Enclosed please find 321$US to be used for the Lord's work among the Khmer refugees in France.

Please continue to win souls to our Lord Jesus Christ while we are waiting for His glorious return and His Kingdom. I am invited today to join our friends and brothers in the new Communist regime. Our parents are well. Please pray for us and for me that one day the Lord will bring me out of Cambodia to serve Him in France and other free countries and meet with you again.

I am going to try my best to get out of the country as the Lord may lead me to do.

Bophana, my darling, please stay true to the Lord Jesus. He is coming soon. Please read your Bible every day and keep on praying for me and our family.

From your husband.[3]

According to a young Christian woman named Nellie, both Chhirc and Voan took refuge until April 21 in the French embassy. On that date, all Cambodians were forced to leave, and Nellie, whose father was French and mother was Cambodian, saw the two men tied up and tossed into the back of a truck that then sped away from the embassy. She never saw them again.

After 1979, some of the Christians who survived the Killing Fields met with the president of World Vision in Kompong Cham for an aid assessment survey. One man reported that he saw Chhirc and Voan in Neak Loeung not many days after April 17, 1975. They were just outside of Phnom Penh, on a road filled with panicked, bewildered people.

It was a scene that repeated itself over and over as the stories began to unfold. Although everyone else tried to blend in because they knew it was safer, these two men stood out in the crowd. They went from person to person, calming them and offering the hope of Christ to anyone who would listen. They handed out tracts, and many people were either so numb or so desperate, they took them. Suddenly, five or six black-clad *cadres* appeared and surrounded Chhirc and Voan. Without any warning, they clubbed both men to death while a stunned crowd looked on.

Two Who Survived

Before I continue the roll call of martyrs, I want to mention two men whose lives impacted my own, especially during the years I spent in the camps. The very thought of these two godly men, the memory of their teaching, and the fact of their friendship encouraged me whenever I felt lonely and isolated.

During the Killing Fields years, and even afterward for a long time, I did not know the fate of these men, or of many believers.

Petros Octavianus was a traveling preacher known as the Billy Graham of Indonesia. He was one of the last men I heard preach at the Khmer Evangelical Church. His words ignited my heart and—although none of us knew it at the time—prepared me for the days ahead. When I later meditated on his words, I knew he understood my circumstances. He had been arrested in Cambodia in 1968. Petros was no stranger to suffering.

Another speaker who preached at the church in Phnom Penh from time to time was Raja Thiagaraja from India. Raja worked with Youth for Christ. In 1974, he arrived at the church somewhat flustered. He was slated to speak at a conference hosted by our church, but no one picked him up at the airport. I was praying at the church when he arrived. Although we'd forgotten him, he was quite gracious. The two of us roomed together, and I was impressed by this godly leader.

His accent was thick and he spoke more rapidly than anyone I'd ever heard, so I was nervous when my three mentors asked me to interpret for him when he preached. The fact that the three of them sat on the front row that night watching my every move didn't help my nerves. I'm not sure I did an adequate job, but every time I looked at the front row, I saw all three men grinning and giving me their thumbs-up.

During the Killing Fields years, and even afterward for a long time, I did not know the fate of these men, or of many believers. These two men lived their lives so completely for the kingdom, I had to assume they were in danger of imprisonment. I knew they, like me, faced the possibility of death every day. Although they survived, to me they were always as good as lost. But their influence remained as a palpable presence in my loneliest hours.

Brother Voan

When something good blooms in my life, I have learned to look for the seed—and from the seed to the person who planted it. Chhirc's cousin Minh Thien Voan planted seeds that thrive today in my own ministry. I never got to thank him adequately.

Voan met Christ in 1962, while he was studying for a master's degree in engineering at the University of Georgia. Although born and raised in Cambodia, he wasn't Khmer. His veins pulsed with Chinese and Vietnamese blood, two strains that marked him as an enemy of the *Angkar* as much as did his faith in Christ.

Like Chhirc, he returned to Cambodia with a fire in his soul for the gospel. Because he was an outspoken witness, he was unable to return to his job with the government. So he found work as an executive for Shell Oil, where he stayed until 1973, when he became first the deputy director, then the director of World Vision.

In the intervening years he attended one of the older churches—Evangelical Church—in Phnom Penh. He influenced many to grow more deeply in Jesus and for a season led this church. Under his guidance, it grew rapidly and became a beacon of light to the city. He also founded an English language school, where many government leaders and students found Christ. When we first met, he was an elder in my church.

Through this godly man I gained a compassion for the poor, the hungry, the needy, and especially for children. He hired me at World Vision and, like Chhirc, entrusted me with leadership responsibilities from the very beginning. He was patient, honest, enduring, and trustworthy.

In those days French was our second language after Khmer. In our schools, English was optional. But Voan encouraged me to gather ten young people who had an intermediate understanding of English and teach them from the gospel of John in English. He seemed to understand that English was on its way to becoming an international language. Because of Voan, when the time came for me to use my English to translate, to interpret, and to communicate as a social worker, I was ready.

March 1975 was a month of monumental highs and lows for Mien Thien Voan. It began with a final visit from Stan Mooneyham. Voan always enjoyed these visits, but this one was bittersweet as the missionaries began packing up to leave the country. He understood, but it was difficult to see them go. The pediatric hospital was almost complete, but it was beginning to look like it might never open. Toward the end of the month, as the political climate of the city heated to a fevered pitch, Mien Thien Voan, whose name means "heavenly messenger," got the best news of his life. His family—his mother, father, and sisters—had given their lives to Christ. His mother had a dream in which she saw Jesus and heard the words, "I died to save you." I can only imagine how encouraging this was to him in his dying moments.

In a letter to his young wife, who was in the United States, Voan wrote, "I might have to die in Cambodia, but it is worth dying when my parents and sisters have turned to Christ. The next time we meet may be in heaven."

Lokrou Sonne

Lokrou is the Khmer rendering of the word *guru*, a title of respect given to a beloved teacher or pastor. Sonne Son's credibility in his life and ministry won him this title among all who knew him. How could I forget the man who helped me buy my first Bible? *Lokrou* Sonne was also my first mentor and hero. I met him just one week after I accepted Christ at the Chaktomuk Conference Hall, where he had translated for Dr. Stan Mooneyham at the evangelistic crusade. He was not only the head of the Khmer Bible Society, he was also an experienced church leader, pastor, and evangelist. Remember my prayer that God would make me a translator of the Bible? *Lokrou* Sonne was not only the reason for that prayer, he was also the beginning of the answer.

Lokrou Sonne and his family almost escaped. They

were given tickets for an Air Cambodge flight out of Cambodia on April 15, 1975. But all flights were canceled on
the 13th, so the tickets were useless. Many who saw
Lokrou Sonne on April 17 have said those familiar words:
"I never saw him again."

Only after 1979 did the fate of *Lokrou* Sonne and his
family become known. Witnesses saw them, along with another Christian family, crossing the Mekong River in a boat.
A violent squall arose and the boat capsized. Most made
it to the shore, but the party was separated for some time.
One by one they began to find each other. To evade arrest
they dressed as peasants and managed to survive the many
purges by local *cadres*. Ultimately, lack of food and sanitation took its toll, and *Lokrou* Sonne and most of his family
members died.[4] Because he introduced me to the eternal
Word of God, *Lokrou* Sonne's influence on my life still re-
verberates. When I returned to Cambodia from Thailand,
almost ten years after his death, I became the chairman
of the same Bible Society he had directed. I have been, as
I prayed I would, involved in several translation projects.
In 1997, Bible Society board members and I enjoyed an
unprecedented two-hour audience with King Norodom
Sihanouk at his royal residence in Siem Reap. We pre-
sented him with a specially bound Khmer Bible. His reaction was one of deep and genuine gratitude. During this
visit, the king shared some of his own story. He was appointed to a puppet role—head of state of Democratic

Kampuchea—by the Khmer Rouge. He and his wife were veritable hostages in his own home in Phnom Penh. Many of his children and grandchildren, like so many of his countrymen, lost their lives during the Killing Fields.

These men, Chhirc, Voan, and Sonne, are just three who represent many. I have already mentioned Chhawn, who died because of his eyeglasses. In the Catholic church, Monsignor Tep Im and Father Jean Badre, along with others, were assassinated. The list of Christians who lost their lives numbers close to ten thousand. Too many to name. Too many about whom we who survived say, "I never saw him again."

The Great Leap Forward

Often the most exotic plants in the world's most beautiful gardens first took root in a greenhouse. In an environment of perfectly controlled heat and moisture, they gather strength for their eventual relocation. Once the plant reaches a certain level of maturity, it is transplanted to its final setting where it can flourish and continue to grow. Want a dramatically lovely plant you can show off to the world? Start in a greenhouse.

The Cambodian church had just such a greenhouse. We weren't meant to stay there, but we were planted there first. Our greenhouse is called Thailand.

In the beginning the Khmer Rouge loved to remind their prisoners that the Cambodians were advancing with a "great leap forward."[5] None of us, as we mustered every morning to tunes inspired by the Chinese Revolution that crackled throughout the camp loudspeakers, could figure out what exactly these words meant. Except that, despite the majestic flourishes of gongs and xylophones, everyone knew they were false. Thousands of dying Cambodians were "building the motherland" on lies.

Meanwhile the church was building upon the lives of men and women and upon the risen Savior they served. *Here* is the hinge-point of my story. This is where the deaths begin to shed their purposeless clothes and don the mantle of meaning. The senseless reveals itself to be sacred after all. Not one of the more than ten thousand Christians died in vain. And those who survived?

It's time to jump ahead for a moment. The church's "great leap forward" wasn't based on lies; it was based on Truth. The Truth. First, the church endured the Killing Fields. From 1975 to 1979 we were isolated from one another yet still related with the unshakable ties of family. When the killing and imprisonments began to subside, small groups of believers met secretively in Phnom Penh. But we still weren't out of danger. News of the fledgling church reached the Khmer Rouge, so my family and I fled to Thailand, the greenhouse of the Cambodian church.

That is where we planted fifteen seedling churches and nourished them in anticipation of a return—which didn't happen until eight years later—to the motherland the Khmer had all but annihilated. Now, after almost a decade, we—myself and the other church planters I trained—have planted more than four hundred churches in Cambodia and beyond. And this church is peopled with, some estimate, more than two thousand former Khmer Rouge leaders and officers who stand as brothers and sisters next to those whose families they murdered.[6] *This* is what one might more accurately call a "great leap forward."

Notes

1. Charles Colson, "The Faith of the Cambodian Martyrs," *The Christian Post,* October 29 2007. www.christianpost.com/article/20071029/the-faith-of-the-cambodian-martyrs.

2. Ibid.

3. "Who was Taing Chhirc?" Cambodia Action. www.saocambodia.org/faqs/837-who-was-chhirc-taing.

4. Colson.

5. Haing Ngor, *Survival in the Killing Fields* (New York: Carroll & Graf, 1987), 222.

6. Colson.

Chapter Eleven

A MOSAIC

The Broken Pieces Find Each Other

I began to feel better. We could eat what we wanted
and when we wanted. We could say whatever we
chose. We were free to criticize, to speak out, to show
anger. We didn't have to be silent if someone else did
something stupid or committed an injustice. The long
darkness was almost over. As we walked through the
forest toward the highway, I began to sing.[1]

—Haing Ngor, in *Survival in the Killing Fields*

For you were called to freedom, brothers. Only do not
use your freedom as an opportunity for the flesh, but
through love serve one another.

—Galatians 5:13

IT **IS** almost impossible for a Westerner to comprehend a life without freedom. That must be why, from time to time, someone—usually someone very young—will say when they hear about the injustices committed by the Khmer Rouge against their own people, "I wouldn't stand for it!" or "I would *do something* about it!" But the hard truth is, justice cannot exist where there are no choices.

When Mit Soeun, his wife, his cousin, and I left for Phnom Penh, we were free for the first time in four years. Free, but not safe. The walk back to the city was dangerous. It was unwise to walk at night because there were *punji* pits on either side of the road with sharpened bamboo stakes at the bottom. Many of the land mine detonators had been washed into plain view by the rains, announcing their ominous presence in the daylight. But no one wanted to take their chances with the mines still hidden in open fields.

As we traveled, we saw signs along the highway, messages scrawled in charcoal on paper or wood and attached to trees. On one, someone wrote that he had survived and was headed east. On another, a woman pleaded with her grown children, if they lived, to find her in Phnom Penh. Others stood sentinel, asking if we had seen a father, a brother, a wife, a child. It's all we could talk about when we met each other on the road in the spring of 1979. Did so-and-so survive? Have you seen my wife? When was the last time you saw my husband?

The heart of our nation had been broken, and now we were struggling to reassemble the remaining pieces. Everyone was looking for someone who was lost. Haing Ngor, author of *Surviving the Killing Fields*, headed toward Battambang when he was released. He observed that this swarm of people in 1979 was quite different from the masses that crowded our highways in 1975. Then we had been a healthy, robust, proud lot. Now we were thin and desperate. But the most extraordinary difference, Ngor said, was this: ". . . in 1975 everyone was afraid of the Khmer Rouge. In 1979 the fear had turned to anger."[2]

The Vietnamese, with their fine-boned, pale faces and red stars emblazoned on their helmets, carried AK-47s as they patrolled the national routes and the smaller roads that led into the cities. These Communists were, like the Khmer Rouge, opposed to commerce, but the soldiers turned a blind eye to the bustle of the open markets that popped up everywhere as people discovered rice (there was plenty of it stored in underground warehouses) and other necessities.

They also turned a blind eye to the savage acts of revenge meted out upon the Khmer Rouge *cadres*. More times than I can count, I saw mobs of Cambodian citizens march up to a group of Viet Cong soldiers—they always stood in groups of two or three—pushing a frightened man or woman whose elbows were tightly tied together with a *kramar* and whose eyes betrayed their terror. In shrill voices the crowds proclaimed this prisoner had been a Khmer Rouge leader, a murderer.

The Vietnamese only nodded and did nothing. And nothing was more than enough. These frenzied crowds would then take turns beating their victim. People lined up to deliver a punch or a kick to their former oppressors. The beatings usually ended with so many hatchet blows or knife slashes that when it was over, the accused was nothing more than pieces of mutilated flesh left to rot on the roadside.

For the first time since April 17, 1975, I had a choice. I could fight back. Or I could protect Mit Soeun, the man who had so faithfully protected me. Surely God intended my newfound freedom for something more noble than revenge. I found some paper and wrote testifying to the fact that Mit Soeun had been a kind, caring officer who never, not once, abused any of us. Before the three hundred men and women of our community dispersed, I asked them for a favor. I listed every one of their names on my petition in pencil (there were no pens). I then mixed the charred insides of used battery cells with oil and made a small vat of black ink. Each of the three hundred supporters pressed a thumb into the ink, then left an imprint next to his or her name, in effect witnessing under oath that our leader was innocent. I gave this petition to Mit Soeun to keep with him. There were so many lives I could not save, but now I could finally *do something.*

How I Found My Mother

Before we traveled very far in our journey, as we crossed a bridge with a throng of others, I heard a woman call my name. My real name.

"Sovann," she said, "your mother survived. I can take you to her and to Ah Mom, your youngest sister. She hasn't left your mother's side these four years."

What a mixture of emotions assaulted me! I was thrilled to learn that my mother and sister had survived. But the implication was clear: no one else in my family had.

I remembered my last conversation with my father. It was the night before I was to lead the Bible conference with Chhirc in Takhmau, four days before the siege of Phnom Penh. From the first days of my conversion to Christ, my father and I had loved to dialogue about matters of faith.

"Son, it looks like the Khmer Rouge will soon take over most of the country," my father said. "As you know, they are opposed to all religions. If they destroy your church buildings and your Bible, if they disrobe your priests . . ."

". . . pastors, Dad."

"Yes, of course, your pastors." He smiled. "If they dismantle it all, can you still worship your God?"

"Dad, just like I've said before; Jesus is in my heart. I can worship Him anywhere. If everything is taken away,

I will worship Him on the back of a water buffalo. I will worship Him in the branches of a tree. I will worship Him while rowing a boat. He is everywhere."

My father, although he was staunchly Buddhist in his beliefs and practices, was a real advocate for his son's Christian faith. He actually encouraged his grandchildren to attend church. World Vision paid me a salary, which I shared with my parents: six thousand riels to my mother and two thousand riels to my father, whose needs were far less than hers. Whenever I sent him cocoa or other gifts, he showed them to the other men in the village, proudly proclaiming, "Look what my son, the Christian, sent to me!"

"Dad," I asked gently, "what if the *wats* and everything in them are destroyed? What if the monks are defrocked? Will you be able to worship then? Will you be able to practice your faith?"

"No, son." He looked away. "It would be impossible. I pay homage to Buddha [he meant the actual statue], to the *dharma* [Buddha's teaching], and to the *sangha* [the monks]. If these things were taken from me, I could not profess my faith. It would be an impossibility."

"If these things happen," I said, not wanting to believe they could, "and if it looks bad, please call on the name of Jesus. Even if it is the last moment of your life."

My father did not respond. Instead he kissed me good-bye, and I never saw him again.

When I met the woman who promised to take me to my mother, it was evening. We decided to spend the night right there. In the morning we followed the woman, who was a distant relative, to her nearby home where my mother and sister were staying. On the way, I heard that my mother was too distraught to return to her own home. Too much there reminded her of the family she had lost. The woman warned us that my mother's eyes had been affected by her continual weeping and by illness. She might not recognize me. This didn't seem possible.

"What can I do for you, sir?" asked the tiny, shriveled woman, who I immediately identified as my dear mother, when we approached. She had no idea who I was. She seemed so fragile, I didn't want to shock her.

Oh Lord, I said quietly with my hand lifted up to heaven, *how can I convince her? She is missing out on some joyful news! Help me make her see.*

"Tell me about each of your children," I said. "Would you please give an account of them?"

I wasn't prepared for the litany of bad news my mother recited. But I knew I had to share this pain with her. One by one she told me how her children—my sisters, half brothers, and half sisters—died. Seven died of starvation or sickness, others less slowly. All of them lived near her, so she knew their stories intimately.

I've already mentioned Boran, my eldest half sister, who had been assigned to grow sweet potatoes in a communal garden. By the time the harvest came, she was so weak and hungry she became bold enough to steal. She kept a few of the smaller sweet potatoes in her pocket. One of the *chhlops* saw her and alerted the *cadres*. A thirteen-year-old officer beat her to death right there in the field. Boran still had the sweet potatoes in her pocket when she died.

Sovannary, a brilliant scholar and teacher, the one who had given me a book of Bible stories so many years ago, lived in a village nearby. The Khmer Rouge had told her they were going to grant her a special favor. Would she like to live with her mother? Her husband, who had been a battalion commander in Lon Nol's army, had already been taken away and killed. She was raising their children alone. And she missed our mother. Oh yes, she would love to live with her mother. When could she go? Right away, they answered. Walk this way with us.

They murdered her on the outskirts of her own village. My sister's crime? She taught French at the local high school. Only one of her children survived.

And my father? He was the first to die. Just months after the siege of Phnom Penh, he died of starvation. To this day, I treasure the hope that he did what I asked him to do—that before he died he called upon the name of Jesus.

"Can you tell me about your seventh child?" I asked. "Did he survive?"

"Oh no, I'm sure not."

"But how do you know?"

"Sovann was our most spoiled child! He was the favorite. He didn't know how to farm or work hard. We weren't hard enough on him." She began to sob. "It's our fault! If my husband and I had raised him like the others—tough—maybe he would have made it."

I stood in front of her and said, "I am Sovann, your son."

She began to cry even harder. "No, don't say that. All of my children have died except for one. Sovann is dead. Don't lie to me. I would rather have no hope at all than false hope."

Again I looked toward heaven and pleaded, *Oh Lord, help me make her see!*

"Your son Sovann was a follower of Jesus Christ. Remember? Surely this Jesus, whom he worshiped, spared his life." I watched the hope flicker in her swollen, red eyes. I stooped before her and gently said, "Mae, I am your son."

From the day I first met Jesus Christ, the Prodigal Son story had been meaningful to me, but I had never grasped its full weight. I stayed with my mother for the next few days, and I am pretty sure she never slept. She was just too excited. She went from house to house, proclaiming to anyone who would listen, "My son is alive!" Her joy was infectious. I think it was this joy that made her willing to return to her home. With Soeun and his wife, I took her there.

On the way she said, "Son, would you please forgive me?"

"Why, Mae?"

"I lost all hope and assumed you were dead."

"I understand," I said. "Of course I forgive you."

"But I wanted to earn merit for you in the next life, so I gave away all of your clothes as alms. There is nothing left of your possessions."

One by one we found each other.
We had been fractured,
but not annihilated; wounded,
but not completely killed;
erased, but our imprint remained;
dimmed, but still visible.

This would have made perfect sense to a devout Buddhist. "Mae, you probably know by now that these things mean nothing to me compared to the joy of finding you."

This, she understood.

How I Found My Wife

I did not stay with my mother. Mit Soeun and his wife lived with her and protected her for a year. But I felt my presence was a burden. She didn't make me feel that way, but each mouth to feed and each body to shelter put more pressure on her. I left her village and lived in and around Phnom Penh, working whatever jobs I could find. At first I joined the crew of a small cargo boat that delivered lead and copper from Phnom Penh to Tan Chau, Vietnam, and then traveled back to Phnom Penh with a load of rice and sweet potatoes. I would land in Phnom Penh on Friday, visit with my twin daughters, and leave again for Vietnam every Monday.

The remaining months of that first year, 1979, were spent wandering, when I could, and locating the survivors I knew. That's basically how the church in Phnom Penh, and possibly in all of Cambodia, formed. One by one we found each other. We had been fractured, but not annihilated; wounded, but not completely killed; erased, but our imprint remained; dimmed, but still visible. Later, I read Paul's description of himself and his fellow leaders in the body of Christ and saw us clearly in his words:

> But we have this treasure in jars of clay, to show that the surpassing power belongs to God and not to us. We are afflicted in every way, but not crushed; perplexed, but not driven to despair; persecuted, but not forsaken; struck down, but not destroyed; always carrying in the body the death of Jesus, so that the life of Jesus may also be manifested in our bodies. (2 Corinthians 4:7–10)

The first Christian I encountered was Sam Ol. He and his mother had lived on the premises of Bethany Church until April 1975. The church grew rapidly in those years, and Sam Ol acted as both security guard and supervisor of the property.

In the interim he had married an educated woman. She encouraged him to reopen the church in 1979 at their home in Phsar Chas near the post office in Phnom Penh. What joy to reunite with Sam Ol in the church where we had spent so many happy times. During the first Sunday service, I met his cousins Yorng Soth, Yorng Kosal, Yorng Sayheng, and Yorng Kimhân. These siblings were the first Cambodian Christians I met at Bethany Church after my conversion in 1972. Many a time during that first year of following Christ, when I had no food to eat, these men graciously shared their food with me.

On the second Sunday I met Pastor Reach Yea. He was one of the greatest preachers I had ever known. Pastor Yea stayed in Phnom Penh and ministered to us for a while before fleeing to Thailand with his family. The Lord used him mightily to strengthen the church among the Cambodian refugees in the camps.

If not for the emotional grief and the physical weakness that lingered, 1979 would have been like a treasure hunt. Like my mother, whenever I discovered someone I had given up for lost, I could hardly contain my joy. Each of these reunions gave me much cause to hope.

But there was one area where I couldn't shake a feeling of hopelessness: marriage. First, I had failed in my relationship with Thavy. I had not been able to marry her properly, and the relationship had floundered and died. I kept wondering what I could have done to be a better husband. I was an utter failure. I couldn't forgive myself. I did not think I was capable of leading the church in any capacity—not with this in my past. Second, for so many reasons I felt no one would want to marry me. I still suffered from an unsightly skin condition. I was weak, malnourished, and barely able to work. I faced a lifetime alone.

In Phnom Penh, I met Sameth, a man who had lived with me in *Wat Saravoan*. He became a Christian in 1972, about the time I did. His father-in-law, Pastor Sieng Ang, had also been a Buddhist monk. During the Killing Fields, Pastor Ang was out of the country. He was the first Cambodian missionary to plant a church among the Khmer Krom people in South Vietnam. He returned to Phnom Penh in 1979 and started an underground church in his house near the former Takhmau Bible School, which had been converted by the new government to a health center.

Although it was risky, Pastor Ang and Sameth traveled to meet with the underground church in all its locations. He was a wise man of great faith. That first year he was arrested for his participation in the church, but released after a few months. I felt an affinity with him because of our shared Buddhist backgrounds and imprisonments. I finally unburdened to Pastor Ang the self-condemnation that plagued me. I will never forget my relief as he explained the Scriptures more fully to me. I was not only forgiven, I was restored. I began to hope again that God could use me. And I began to pray for a godly wife.

I met Boury at an underground church in Sam Ol's house. Four years older than me, she worked in a health center. Like all government workers during this time, she was not paid in money because none was available but in rice, salt, salted fish, and milk powder. Boury regularly visited the sick and needy—a large proportion in Cambodia at the time—and shared her "salary" with them. This impressed me.

One day I offered her a lift on my bicycle. She said she could get medicine that would cure the ringworm on my face. She was as good as her word, and before long my face was clear! I discovered she was a widow—her husband had been a nursing teacher in Lon Nol's army—with six children. At first I thought she merely pitied me. But as our relationship deepened, I began to wonder if Boury was the one.

For the past four years, whenever I called on the Holy Spirit to guide me, He did. I had come to trust implicitly in God's sovereign will for my life. I asked God to make it crystal clear whether Boury was to be my wife. When it came to women, I trusted Him more than I trusted me!

I knew He would not answer me audibly or pierce the sky with His hand and point with His finger, but I believed He would show me in no uncertain terms.

I said, "Lord, if Boury is the one You plan to bless me with as my wife, would You let her invite me to her home for a meal?" Not just any meal but *char trakuon*, a meal I had eaten often when food was plentiful in *Wat Saravoan*. And not just once, but I asked the Lord to cause Boury to serve this same meal three times in a row. *Char trakuon* (known as fried *kangkung* among the Chinese) is a simple, inexpensive dish of fried morning glory with salted black soybean. When I lived with my uncle in *Wat Saravoan*, I ate *bawbaw* (rice porridge) and *char trakuon* every morning for breakfast. If a woman wanted to impress me, *char trakuon* would probably not be what she chose to serve. But a woman of good sense just might.

Boury lived with her older brother Kun in Chamkar Mon, an affluent neighborhood in Phnom Penh near the Monivong Bridge. The house had originally been owned by a European ambassador. A sprawling bungalow with many rooms, it boasted a large garden with a variety of trees and plants. It was also very near the warehouse where the bag of rice fell at my feet like a gift in 1975.

Kun was a commander with the Ministry of National Defense. As is common in our culture, her older brother Kun stepped in to take the place of Boury's father after their parents died when she was very young. The Ministry of Defense owned the home, and Kun was respected by everyone who knew him. He was, however, living a homosexual lifestyle.[3] But he loved to care for those around him and shared his home freely. Boury invited me over to this home for dinner. That night she served me *char trakuon*. Twice more she asked me to dine in her home and both times, you guessed it, she served *char trakuon*.

This could only be God's direction. Kun was known for his skills as a gourmet chef. He owned and operated a restaurant on his property (where I later worked as a waiter) that had become famous locally for its cuisine, especially his celebrated minced beef noodle soup. When I approached my future brother-in-law to ask for his sister's hand in marriage, he—to my dismay—discouraged me. But when he explained why he thought Boury was unsuitable as wife material, I was relieved. This was a problem I could definitely fix. Kun felt the limited scope of Boury's culinary skills might prove frustrating after a few months of marriage. Did I realize the only thing she could cook was *char trakuon, nothing but char trakuon?* I said, "This is the woman I want! I can teach her everything I know."

I asked Boury to marry me. She was ready to accept but wanted to consult her six children. Five of them readily gave their blessing, all but Kanika. Because she did not yet know me well, she doubted my sincerity. I'm not sure what tipped the scale in my favor, but two weeks later Kanika changed her mind.

We were married on April 16, 1980, in a small, simple ceremony at her uncle's home with a few close relatives and friends surrounding us. A year later we had a baby girl. We named her for something we were slowly beginning to enjoy: shalom, or peace.

How I Found My Calling

A. W. Tozer said, "Without worship, we go about miserable." For Cambodian Christians during this tragic period, misery was a tempting option. Although many of the elderly Buddhist monks who survived the Killing Fields were allowed to be reordained, and although the remaining Cham people (the Muslim minority) were recognized by the government, Christians were still considered the enemy. At our National Assembly in 1980, some members of parliament represented the Buddhist and Cham communities, but there were none to represent the Christians. In everyone's minds, Christians were still associated with the West. No one could forget the American bombing raids or the Western backing of Lon Nol against our beloved Prince Sihanouk.

A few missionaries, usually connected with the relief efforts of NGOs (nongovernmental organizations), trickled back into the country, but they were put on a very short leash. Reverend Jean Clavaud of Oikoumene was continually under surveillance by the new government. The two of us became friends, and I learned a lot from his boldness. Clavaud kept an office in his room at the Samaki Hotel and answered to the Ministry of Foreign Affairs for his activities. But he was hardly ever in this office.

Every day he traveled throughout the city distributing Bibles. He usually rode in a *remorque*, a small cart that could hold up to four passengers, pulled by a bicycle. I often pedaled the bicycle for him. (Only the *cadres* in the new government had cars.) He placed a Bible, sometimes two, in his *sarong*, giving it away to any Christian he met. Eventually in 1984, he was deported. Though by then we should have been accustomed to loss, we felt it deeply and grieved at the departure of this brave brother.

Whether local or foreign, we Christians were *persona non grata*. Who would blame us if we succumbed to the pull of despair? But somehow, I knew there was an alternative to misery—and I knew that alternative was worship.

That doesn't mean I felt a personal responsibility to lead in this area. I most certainly did not. But I felt the need for the Christians in our small churches—usually no more than twenty at a time, meeting in three scattered locations—to exalt the Lord in worship. Perhaps that's why an article I read one day stirred my heart. Someone had smuggled in a magazine, called *Open Doors*, and it eventually made its way to me. It was published by Brother Andrew, a Christian leader famous for his ministry to the persecuted church. The story that grabbed my attention was about two young men who were sent to a psychiatric hospital for composing and leading worship music for the underground church in Russia. I couldn't help but admire their boldness. Before being transported to the hospital, they performed some of their music for their fans, who were all young Communists.

"Listen to our music. Do you think this is the work of a psychotic? Can a madman create such harmony?"

"No!" shouted the crowd.

"Do you believe I am insane?" said one of the men.

"No!" was again the answer.

I had had no training or experience.
I could not play an instrument.
How could I be used
to lead people to worship?

There was no reprieve. The men were immediately taken to a psychiatric hospital. But their music was instrumental in bringing many young people, including some members of the KGB, to Christ. In spite of their circumstances—circumstances I certainly identified with—they proclaimed their Savior in worship and led others to do the same.

I was alone in our home and began to wonder who

could fill this vital role in our country. It would take strong leadership. Creativity. Resources. All things the Cambodian church did not have then. I began to pray, "Lord, who will lead the church in Cambodia to worship You now?"

"*You.*"

I wondered if the still, small voice I heard was really God's. Such a humorous thought. Surely I misunderstood. I was not fit for this task. I was not born into a musical family. I had had no training or experience. I could not play an instrument. How could I be used to lead people to worship? So I asked the Lord again, three times in all: "Who will You use in Cambodia to lead people to worship You?"

And every time I heard the same answer: "*You.*"

While I was praying and wondering how this strange calling from the Lord was going to take place, Boury came home. I shared it with her, expecting her to get a good laugh out of the crazy notion. Unlike the two Russian musicians, at that moment I didn't have much confidence in my own sanity.

"You will be a good musician." She stopped to peer more closely at me. "No, a gifted musician! And I will find a way to pay for the best teachers available."

Boury's blessing was exactly what I needed. First, we found a well-known Cambodian flautist and composer, who agreed to teach me. Mr. Yin Dikan introduced me to Mr. Sothyvann, a guitarist who is still famous in

Cambodia. God continued to open doors, doors I never knew existed. I met Mr. Hong Phat, a German-educated composer who taught me to write songs.[4] Finally, Mr. Chanthou, director of a national music recording program, taught me what I needed to know about producing music.

In the beginning I just learned all I could—as quickly as I could. And as secretively. We usually met in restaurants for breakfast for my first lesson of the day. Most often, we met in Kun's restaurant next door. The lessons with each man typically lasted no more than fifteen to thirty minutes, one after the other, so we wouldn't raise any suspicions. But we met every day.

Mr. Dikan was clever not just musically. He taught me music theory using the white tablecloth and a toothpick dipped in the dark, strong tea in his cup. After two years of continual, daily lessons, I was able to not only play the guitar, the bamboo flute, and other indigenous instruments of our country, but I could also write music. God had written a purpose on my heart, and that purpose began to swell into song. Apart from watching the gospel touch others' lives, nothing has given me more joy than making music for my Lord. And nothing has caused me quite so much trouble.

Later, while living in Thailand, I discovered that a culture's vitality and identity is linked to its music. As a refugee church, we not only worshiped, we also performed and produced music in the traditional Khmer style and shared that music with fellow refugees. For eight years, although God did not yet return us to our country, He used the church to return the country's music to us.

Notes

1. Haing Ngor, *Survival in the Killing Fields* (New York: Carroll & Graf, 1987), 377.

2. Ibid., 389.

3. Years later, Kun became a follower of Jesus. He renounced his former life and committed himself to Christ fully. He died in 2005.

4. Mr. Hong Phat later became Pastor Bin David of New Jerusalem Church in Phnom Penh. Together, we put together the largest band and choir ever gathered in Cambodia to celebrate "Jesus 2000" at the Olympic Stadium.

Chapter Twelve

THE MUSIC
RESOUNDS

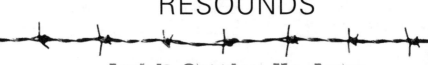

And It Carries Me Away

Above all sing spiritually. Have an eye to God in every
word you sing. Aim at pleasing him more than yourself,
or any other creature. In order to do this attend strictly
to the sense of what you sing, and see that your heart
is not carried away with the sound, but offered to
God continually; so shall your singing be such as the
Lord will approve here, and reward you
when he cometh in the clouds of heaven.

—John Wesley

I put my trust in You.
In this time of need, dear Lord Jesus, help me.
I am lost in a big sea.
Guide me and lead me ashore for my safety.
In the midst of storms,
I'm secure for You are with me.
Hold my hand and lead me through.
Do hold my hand and lead me through.

—Barnabas Mam

WHILE I was not born into a musical family, I was intimately familiar with a similar aspect of our country's culture. Although music remained a mystery to me until 1980, poetry was deeply ingrained in me in my childhood.

My mother taught me to chant Cambodian poetry. Early on, I preferred Khmer poetry over prose because of its structure and sound. It's quite complicated, a lot like music. To Cambodians, the more patterns and variations in a poem, the better. These patterns are constructed with intricate syllable meters and rhyming. For example, in the *"Patya Vat"* meter, one of many patterns, the fourth syllable of the second line must rhyme with the end syllable of the first line—and the end syllable of the third line must rhyme with the end syllable of the second line. When there is more than one stanza, the end syllable of the first line of the new stanza must rhyme with the end syllable of the fourth line of the previous stanza.

Written and chanted poetry is a rich part of Cambodian culture. And, in less than five years, the Khmer Rouge had almost eradicated it. Not only did we bear witness to the death of our loved ones, we also watched the death of our culture and its beauty as expressed in all of our art forms, including poetry and music.

At first, my new musical skills were born into a vacuum. Each time I wrote a song, I sang it to an audience of one. Sometimes three, when Boury and Shalom were around to listen. In those days caution was my middle name. None of us could carry a new Bible or hymnal in public. If caught, the authorities would assume we'd gotten it from a foreigner. We were not allowed any contact with outsiders—especially missionaries—who in the minds of the government might as well be CIA agents.

It was a lonely, isolated time. Little by little, the church formed and met whenever we could in three locations in and around Phnom Penh; one in the large basement of Boury's brother's home, another in Sam Ol's house church in Phnom Penh, a third in Pastor Ang's house church in Takhmau in Kandal Province. The maximum number we could gather in one place was twenty.

I developed a dream.
Wouldn't it be a miracle
if my songs could be sung
by twenty people, all at once,
in each of the churches?

We developed some little rituals out of necessity. Each week each house church leader sent a verbal message to the believers, telling them which location to go to next Sunday morning. For safety's sake, we did not meet at the same place every time. We moved from place to place.

Each shepherd also gave his flock a Scripture reference to read, usually something from the New Testament and a psalm or proverb. During the week we memorized these texts so we could recite them together at the meeting. We met for two hours during our Sunday service.

Whenever I taught in our home, I spoke both in Khmer and English to help those who were keen to learn English. Some of the younger, new believers could travel from place to place, but not me. I was known.

One of these new converts was Uong Rien, a young and zealous officer in the militia who accompanied Pastor Ang when he did house visits. Uong Rien was introduced to me and expressed his desire to learn to play the guitar. We met for lessons twice every week. Uong Rien later became one of the first Cambodian church leaders, founding Open Gate Christian Fellowship in Phnom Penh. He still serves in that church as senior pastor.

I kept writing songs and singing them. Before long, I developed a dream. Wouldn't it be a miracle, a wonderful work of God, if my songs could be sung by twenty people, all at once, in each of the churches? After four years of harsh reality, I'd forgotten those rainy days at Sambok Moan where I could envision the entire world singing "How Great Thou Art" together. The dimensions of my dream had diminished, but the vision was essentially the same. I longed to see the body of Christ in her bright, clean robes of righteousness, singing her heart out as one.

I decided to share some of my songs with a few trusted friends. Their response was anything but encouraging:

"Don't dare write any more Christian music to Cambodian tunes!"

"This music is too sad. It reminds us of everything sad about our past. It doesn't encourage us, not at all."

"You are a son of the devil," a few even said to my face. "You are bringing the satanic culture to the church of God."

It was enough to make me want to give up. Then I received the letter from Alice.

Son of Encouragement

Alice Compain was one of four Overseas Mission Fellowship (OMF) missionaries who responded to Major Chhirc Taing's appeal to Western believers at the Keswick Convention in England in 1973. A year later, she arrived in Phnom Penh. She was evacuated not many months after that, but not before we became friends and coworkers. And now she was in Bangkok, working with Cambodian refugees. She wrote to me with a simple request: Could I send her some praise and worship songs set to Cambodian tunes? She knew such music may not exist, so she asked:

Could you find a talented musician to write this kind of music for us? The church in the refugee camp on the border is struggling to sing the old, translated hymns. The tunes are unfamiliar and the tempo only frustrates them. Many are common people who have never been exposed to Western culture. Can you help us? We desperately need songs with solid Christian truth written in the Cambodian style.

I sent her a collection of my songs, but didn't tell her who had written them. Before putting them in the mail—which in itself was a dangerous undertaking—I asked my music tutors to look over everything and make sure the melodies were true to our traditions.

They had nothing but praise for the music, but warned me that I was committing treason by communicating with someone outside Cambodia. At just the right time, as I was preparing to post the documents and wondering how I could do it safely, I met Daniel, a Cambodian Catholic believer who worked at the Samaki Hotel. The Samaki was the only hotel in Phnom Penh where relief organization staff members were allowed to stay. Because he worked there, Daniel was able to smuggle my letters with their precious musical content to Bangkok.

Alice responded quickly, as quickly as mail moved in those days, and thanked me profusely for the music. I decided to tell her I was the composer. The third time I heard from Alice, she suggested I use another name in our letters, so my family and the church would be safe if our letters were ever intercepted. She thought the name *Barnabas*, which means "son of encouragement," would be the perfect pseudonym because my songs had provided the Cambodians in Thailand with so much encouragement.

The moment I saw the name in her letter, I received it as a gift. It confirmed the unexpected call on my life to lead our people in worship. From that time on, I was Barnabas Mam. Later, when I arrived at Site II refugee camp in Thailand, I decided to register with UNBRO (United Nations Border Relief Operations) using this new name. My mother, sister, and other extended family were still in Cambodia, and I did not want to cause them any harm. I have been Barnabas ever since.

Our goal was to compose music that stayed true to the ancient forms and to write words that reflected solid biblical theology and values.

The next time Alice wrote, there was a bulky envelope stuffed inside hers. A Cambodian songwriter named Sam Sarin[1] wrote:

Brother, I don't know if you are older or younger than me. I do know you have known the Lord longer than I have. I now have a collection of your songs and I am convinced you are a gifted songwriter. Can we work together as a team? Please kindly proofread my songs that I have enclosed. Feel free to make any corrections or comments about them. I believe, together, we can compose the first ever Cambodian hymnbook.

It was a match made in heaven. I continued to write songs and make minor changes to the ones Sarin wrote and sent to me. He did the same with mine. I worked in obscurity in Cambodia, trying to be productive without endangering my family or the underground church. Sarin worked much more freely in the Khao I Dang refugee camp in Thailand. Alice served as our musical adviser.

My mother's instruction in Khmer poetry came in handy during this time. Our goal was to compose music that stayed true to the ancient forms she had taught me in my youth and to write words that reflected solid biblical theology and values. But while the traditional melodies gave the refugee church a sense of home and familiarity, using them caused some problems. The younger generation didn't know the tunes their elders knew so well. While we provided the name of the original melody with each song, this didn't always help people sing them accurately, or at all. The church needed to *hear* the songs.

Until then, my music made, of necessity, a quiet sound in my own city. In fact in the local underground church, it was virtually silent. But the exiled saints in Thailand needed to listen to its melodies. And the only way to amplify the sound loud enough for their ears to hear was to record the songs. And for that, we needed a recording studio.

Breaking the Silence

It was an absurd idea. My own friends still weren't so sure my music was a good idea. We had worked so hard to make music the way music ought not to be made: soundlessly. But it was time to change all of that.

Culture was making a tentative comeback in Cambodia. In 1983 there were only three known musical groups in all of the country: one connected with the National Radio, another with the Ministry of Culture, and the other with the Ministry of National Defense. Mr. Chanthou, my friend with the Ministry of Culture, and the three men who taught me flute, guitar, music theory, and songwriting again offered their expertise. We had already grown to love each other deeply. I am forever indebted to these gracious, talented men. Even so, what happened next can only be considered a miracle.

Through Mr. Chanthou we acquired a brand-new

Yamaha mixer with sixty-four channels and a synthesizer. Mr. Yin Dikan, Mr. Sothyvann, and Mr. Hong Phat, along with our friend Chanthou, gathered the musicians. These men were not believers (Hong Phat later gave his life to Christ), but they agreed to help me produce my music. This endeavor was not without danger, and the men, who were savvy enough to know that, must have counted the cost before agreeing to help.

Boury watched as our bedroom was transformed into a recording studio. First, we moved the bed out. Then we hung heavy curtains over the lighter ones already there to filter out any outside noise and, in our unique situation, to ensure no one on the outside heard us. Then we moved in the equipment and I worked to assemble it, turn its many settings to their proper places, and translate the English instructions for the two volunteer sound engineers.

Then one by one, the musicians showed up. We used a blend of indigenous and Western instruments, including the *Khim*, our version of the Chinese sitar; a two-stringed instrument called the *Takhe* (crocodile), so named because it looks like a sleeping crocodile; a Khmer xylophone called the *Roneat*; and the *Kloy*, or bamboo flute.

In one night in 1983 we recorded fourteen songs for our first album, then two more albums the next year. What we were doing was patently illegal, so we started at 10:00 p.m. and made sure we were finished by 4:00 a.m.

That way fewer people noticed the trickle of people into Kun's house. We lived in the military district of the capital city, not tucked away in an obscure village. The recording for each album took place in one night only; any longer would put everyone at greater risk. We played each song through four times and later chose the one that sounded the best. No rehearsals. No starting over.

As you may imagine, an element of fear crackled in the atmosphere during these clandestine sessions. Boury and others spent the long night in another part of the house. They weren't sleeping or trying to avoid our music. They prayed. Their top prayer request was that the electricity would work! Twenty-four-hour electricity was not something anyone in Phnom Penh could rely on then. We had a generator, but if we cranked it up in the middle of the night, we would be sure to draw spies to our home.

The Nucleus of the Underground Church

Bit by bit, the church began to stabilize, though we never met without the knowledge that we could be arrested on any given Sunday. On the night years ago when I went to the crusade at Chaktomuk Hall and gave my life to Jesus Christ, an acquaintance named Paulerk Sar was also there. He heard the gospel, but he did not respond to it. Later, after the evacuation of Phnom Penh, I knew we were both in the Prey Veng Province at the same time, but we never saw one another. I knew a little of

Paulerk's past—he had studied law before the Killing Fields—but I didn't know him well.

Then I heard he had become a Christian and wanted to see me. I was skeptical. Could I trust him? What if he was a spy? I remembered that I had tried to pretend I was a Christian on that fateful night six years before. My goal had been to report the names of leaders back to my Communist mentor. What if Paulerk was doing the same? Despite my misgivings, I decided to meet him. But there was no peace; instead I felt a heavy dread.

The moment we locked eyes and shook hands, the heaviness disappeared. Here was my brother! Paulerk, like me, acquired a new name in the underground church. He became Paul, and in 1994 he became the first chairman of the Bible Society in Cambodia and, two years later, the first chairman of the Evangelical Fellowship of Cambodia.

The two of us bonded immediately. My friends from earlier days in the church, Timothy and Peter,[2] joined Paul and me in a tight-knit group. After I began corresponding with Alice Compain, Daniel—the man at the Samaki Hotel who handled all the sensitive mail—also became part of this influential set of friends. Timothy attended an English class I taught in Chamkar Mon and, after class, collected my mail for Daniel. Peter worked at the Phnom Penh River Port where he met some foreign, believing sailors. These men smuggled Khmer Bibles to Peter, which he gave to the Christian survivors in the city.

To live in Phnom Penh, at least one member of every household was required to work for the government of what was now called the People's Republic of Kampuchea (PRK). Boury, her children, and I were fine because of Kun's job. Paul's father worked for a government hospital, so Paul was allowed to stay . . . until his father died. Thankfully, he was offered several jobs and accepted one as a member, essentially a secret agent, of the Vietnamese intelligence agency in Phnom Penh. Soon God used this strategic placement of my friend to protect me and my family. Whenever Paul learned new information that affected any of us, he passed it along. And usually the news wasn't good.

I was going to be arrested. Paul could only delay the inevitable, so he advised me that I should make my escape sooner rather than later. I sent a set of the master tapes of our three albums to FEBC (Far East Broadcasting Company) Radio in the Philippines and kept another set for myself.

One afternoon, Paul relayed an urgent message that I needed to leave right away, within the next twenty-four hours. But I could not leave openly; no one could in those days. There was only one place for a man like me to go. I could not take Boury or our children, not yet. Our family would have to go incrementally, as well as furtively, if we were to keep from arousing suspicion. It was time to go where my songs had gone, to Thailand.

Notes

1. Sam later became a pastor of the Cambodian Australian Fellowship in Melbourne, Australia.

2. Peter later became a UN official and an elder of an international church in Bonn, Germany.

Chapter Thirteen

SURVIVING
THE QUESTIONS

Finding God's Love
in the Darkness

Death may be the greatest
of all human blessings.

—Socrates

To say that God loves me is a familiar
notion indeed, but to pursue, know and
experience His love is a rare preoccupation.

—Dana Candler

When you and I hurt deeply, what we really need is
not an explanation from God but a revelation of God.
We need to see how great God is;
we need to recover our lost perspective on life.
Things get out of proportion when we are suffering,
and it takes a vision of something bigger than
ourselves to get life's dimensions adjusted again.

—Warren W. Wiersbe

I have loved you with an everlasting love;
therefore I have continued my faithfulness to you.

—Jeremiah 31:3

DOES GOD love me more than these?"

Whether I could admit it, this was the deeper issue behind my other question, the one I could not avoid: "Why did I live when they did not?"

I suppose this is the natural question of the survivor, but that doesn't make the struggle to find answers any easier. I wondered about these things many times during the four years of Pol Pot's stranglehold on Cambodia, a grip that took the lives of so many. So many lives, but not mine.

Half a million citizens of Phnom Penh, but not me.

My Communist mentor, Mr. At Veth, but not me.

The men I buried at Sambok Moan, but not me.

Chhirc Taing, Mien Thien Voan, *Lokrou* Sonne, but not me.

My brothers and sisters, but not me.

My father, but not me.

I Never Saw Him Again

I have already recounted the first leg of my journey from Phnom Penh to Thailand. My stepson-in-law, a musician friend, and I traveled, disguised as soldiers, without incident to Sihanoukville and from there to the fishing village of Kampenh. In Kampenh we met my trusted friend Mee who was to take us by boat to Laem Son.

I have described the night when we were arrested at sea by the Vietnamese patrol and taken back to Sihanoukville. This experience caused the questions, "Why me?"

and "Why them?" again to echo in my mind. During our interrogation, an accident occurred near the makeshift police station. We heard the collision of a train with a car—a deafening, disturbing noise. The officers left us—giving us an opportunity to escape, which we didn't take—and returned only to release us.

Even then we considered this interruption a gift from the Lord. When they returned, our captors were distracted and seemed less willing to punish us. They considered our situation more reasonably than they had thirty minutes before, and more mercifully. Before letting us go, the officer informed us that our arrest had been, in fact, a rescue. The storm at sea claimed many lives that night. We were inexperienced seamen in a tiny boat. (My friend Mee wanted to wait a day for a larger one, but I insisted on going that night in the only boat available.) We should have died. How many times have I said that? *I should have died.*

After our arrest and release, Mee helped us travel to Laem Son, where we thanked him and bid him good-bye. And once again, I must say the words *I never saw him again.* Mee's wife became ill a few months later. He took her, along with their entire family, to a hospital in Phnom Penh. On the way there the Khmer Rouge—which still prowled in parts of the country, but like a lion missing some of its teeth—launched a bazooka attack, destroying Mee's jeep and killing Mee and every member of his family. I was still alive, and they were gone.

The Questions Persist

Did God love me more than He loved my friends?

We who remained in the wake of so many deaths couldn't help but wonder. On the border between Thailand and Cambodia, an entire dispossessed nation—500,000 of us—huddled in refugee camps with some version of the same question haunting our thoughts. Thailand was where Cambodians who should have died went to live. To survive.

> In Thailand I began to ask in earnest, "Lord, why did I survive? Why did they die?
> Do You love me more than these?"

In times of suffering, perspective is often elusive. Time stands still. It's a paradox, really. Time freezes when you suffer as so many of us did in Cambodia. But add another ingredient to the mix—crisis—and it feels as if you can never stop moving. Our escape to Thailand was a continuation of what I had experienced during the Killing Fields: suffering *and* crisis. I had an odd sense that though life was frozen in time, I could never stop moving forward as if my life depended on it.

Although the deeper questions about God and why He chooses some to survive and some to die haunted the recesses of my mind, the malaise such questions create didn't hit until we were relatively safe in Thailand.

I was no longer on the run, no longer separated from my loved ones, no longer in continual physical pain. Time began to thaw, and the days began to move forward at a more normal pace. I was, perhaps for the first time, still. That's when the questions, once whispered and ignored, began their full frontal assault. So it was in Thailand that I began to ask in earnest, "Lord, why did I survive? Why did they die? Do You love me more than these?"

One thing everyone knows about death is that it is inevitable. Even so, when life is a little bit hard, we might smile and say, "This is better than the alternative," meaning at least I'm not dead. But what is the alternative to death, either now or in the future? Eternal life *here*? A continual, unending existence in a broken, sinful world? That doesn't sound appealing. Maybe the only way to really understand death is to look at what God has to say about it, beginning with the first two people who experienced it.

Adam and Eve must have known immediately that something was wrong in their world. Why else would they have hidden from God after they ate the fruit from the Tree of the Knowledge of Good and Evil? Maybe they hadn't known what the consequences would be, but they

knew their once-perfect world was broken—and they had
broken it.

They couldn't see the future, but God could. So He
offered them the hope of a repair before they even fully
understood their need for one. Genesis 3 is where we find
the first hint that this present life of suffering and sin will
one day be redeemed in Christ. God said to the serpent,
"He shall bruise your head, and you shall bruise his heel"
(Genesis 3:15). Scholars refer to this passage as the *Proto
Evangelium*, the first glimpse of the coming Savior.

Then, once Adam and Eve were well outside of Eden,
covered by the skins of animals God slaughtered for them,
both feet planted in the same shattered world in which we
now live, God did even more than offer hope for a different future. He didn't just suggest to Adam and Eve that
all would be made right in a few thousand years. He protected them—and us—from an *eternal lifetime* of sin and
suffering:

> Then the Lord God said, "Behold, the man has be-
> come like one of us in knowing good and evil. Now,
> lest he reach out his hand and take also of the tree of
> life and eat, and live forever—" therefore the Lord
> God sent him out from the garden of Eden to work
> the ground from which he was taken. He drove out
> the man, and at the east of the garden of Eden he
> placed the cherubim and a flaming sword that turned

every way to guard the way to the tree of life." (Genesis 3:22–24)

As always, God's restrictions are for our good. Live forever in an awkward, separated, dysfunctional relationship with God and with each other? Eternal life upon ground so cursed it can run red with the blood of the Killing Fields?

That's the alternative to death. But that's an alternative God loves us too much to leave us with. So He cordoned off the Tree of Life. For a while. Death isn't the curse of Genesis 3; it is the provision. It is the temporary solution to the eternal problem we brought on ourselves by our sin. It is an expression of God's mercy. The Tree of Life—the antidote to death—was closed to us, locked up tight. But God hasn't forgotten it. One day He will reopen the way to the Tree of Life:

He who has an ear, let him hear what the Spirit says to the churches. To the one who conquers I will grant to eat of the tree of life, which is in the paradise of God. (Revelation 2:7)

Blessed are those who wash their robes, so that they may have the right to the tree of life and that they may enter the city by the gates. (Revelation 22:14)

If I look at it this way, my original question gets turned upside down. Instead of asking, "Does God love me more than these?" maybe I should ask, "Does God love *them* more than *me*?" It might look that way. My friends who died didn't have to escape to Thailand. They were afforded the early escape of heaven. Some were sick and died. Some were beaten and died. Some were killed quickly. In every case, death might be considered a better alternative to suffering.

But isn't that a small consolation, especially given the torturous nature of these deaths? The fact that they died doesn't mean they didn't suffer. Many endured a long prelude of suffering before they died. Unlike Moses' death, which may seem unfair because God took him before he could enter the Promised Land, these deaths ultimately ushered people into heaven only after they experienced extreme agony. Yet if we really think about Moses' death from a holistic, biblical perspective, we're reminded that death isn't a cheat, it's a gift. Maybe the question is not *Why did God allow them to die and me to live?* But, rather, *Where is God's love in the midst of something as ghastly as the Killing Fields?*

Moses may not offer a complete answer but Jesus does. The cross is the only way I can make sense of suffering. C. H. Spurgeon said, "No scene in sacred history ever gladdens the soul like the scene on Calvary . . . Nowhere does the soul find such consolation as on that very spot where misery reigned, where woe triumphed, where agony reached its climax."[1]

In 1972 I met Jesus at the cross. Because I knew His suffering and death were for me, I could comprehend a love so deep it undergirds the deepest wounds, even as they are being inflicted. As Warren Wiersbe says, "When you and I hurt deeply, what we really need is not an explanation from God but a revelation of God."[2]

I had come to know God's love in this way—personally, intimately. No amount of theological wrangling could convince me He did not love me. His favor, those pinpoints of light in the darkness, proved His love. His Spirit, speaking to me when I needed to hear Him most, proved it. The many people who offered me aid, often to their own peril, proved it. Just as my father had said, "Show it to me in writing," when, as a new Christian, I first explained the gospel to him, the whole counsel of Scripture proved God's love.

And if I had died along the way? His love and eternal provision would have been finally and fully realized.

I had been grasped by a God who loved me as dearly as He loved everyone else. Could my survival prove He did not love me? No. Could their deaths prove He did not love them? No. His love was too tenacious to deny. It was inescapable:

> Who shall separate us from the love of Christ? Shall tribulation, or distress, or persecution, or famine, or

nakedness, or danger, or sword? As it is written, "For your sake we are being killed all the day long; we are regarded as sheep to be slaughtered." No, in all these things we are more than conquerors through him who loved us. For I am sure that neither death nor life, nor angels nor rulers, nor things present nor things to come, nor powers, nor height nor depth, nor anything else in all creation, will be able to separate us from the love of God in Christ Jesus our Lord. (Romans 8:35–39)

The danger in telling my story is twofold. Sometimes the mantle of suffering I have woven can seem so heavy, it smothers the message of God's love. At other times my assurances of God's love and favor can make it seem as if the suffering was less horrible than it really was. Neither extreme is true. God's love doesn't negate suffering, and suffering doesn't negate God's love.

In the days and years to come,
God would use my personal agonies
to minister peace to others,
including my own children.

But this tension—between suffering and God's love—can never be seen as a balancing act where each side carries equal weight and each gets equal billing. At the risk of sounding glib, it is important to realize the ultimate winner is God's love. His love triumphed over all and in all. It still does.

His love is triumphant, but it is also mysterious. Dietrich Bonhoeffer, who ultimately died a martyr's death in Nazi Germany, contemplated the mystery of God's love as his nation crumbled and many who seemed so promising lost their lives:

> Who can comprehend how those whom God takes so early are chosen? Does not the early death of young Christians always appear to us as if God were plundering his own best instruments in a time in which they are most needed? Yet the Lord makes no mistakes. Might God need our brothers for some hidden service on our behalf in the heavenly world? We should put an end to our human thoughts, which always wish to know more than they can, and cling to that which is certain. Whomever God calls home is someone God has loved.[3]

My struggle to make peace with the inscrutability of God's love and the horror of those years—a struggle that very nearly sank me once I made it safely to Thailand—

was in itself evidence of God's love for me and those like me. In the days and years to come, God would use my personal agonies to minister peace to others, including my own children. Before long, as half a million of my own people limped across the border and made their way to the camps, I learned it wasn't enough to find refuge within human boundaries like barbed-wire fences and heavily guarded checkpoints.

I desperately needed the palpable refuge of God's love to be really secure. And so did many others.

Refuge, Anything But

In 1989, some fourteen million refugees, victims of famine, war, or both, lived in detention camps worldwide.[4] For eight years, the place that Boury, Kanika, Sokunaroat, Shalom, and I settled into and called home was Site II, the largest of many camps on the Thailand/Cambodia border.

Site II was flat and dry, with just a few trees between the rows of bamboo thatched huts that crowded inside the barbed wire. The four square miles were marked off with a grid of red clay roads and connecting dirt paths. With the crowds of people—sometimes several families living under one small roof—and the emerging commerce between refugees, Site II felt a little like a bustling urban center. And it was only marginally safe. The incidence of violent crime was high.

The border camps were controlled by different political factions, including the Vietnamese and the Khmer
Rouge. For the Thai government, we were a human
"buffer zone," our presence shielding their country from
a frontal attack from Cambodia. That didn't mean we
were never attacked. Many of us slept with our bags
packed in case we had to evacuate because of heavy
shelling. Our daughters and I developed a pattern that
would have seemed routine had the times not been so
perilous. Kanika, Sokunaroat, and Shalom knew that
three light taps on their backsides meant they must wake
immediately. If we didn't leave the house, they would lie
flat on the floor, each girl beneath her bed, until Boury
and I gave the all-clear signal. From 1982 to 1984, there
were eighty-five evacuations, almost all of them during
shelling attacks.[5] Multiply my experience nearly 150,000
times over and you can imagine the collective history of
such a place. So many memories in one crowded setting.
So many people stunned that we had made it there, that
we were alive. No wonder suicide and depression were
rampant. This is what awaited us in Thailand. But first,
we had to get there. What we expected would be a one-
or two-month journey took almost a year.

Notes

1. Charles Haddon Spurgeon, www.spurgeon.org/sermons/0126.
   htm.

2. Warren W. Wiersbe, http://dailychristianquote.com/dcqwiersbe.
   html.

3. Eric Metaxas, *Bonhoeffer: Pastor, Martyr, Prophet, Spy* (Nashville: Thomas Nelson, 2010), 383.

4. James F. Lynch, "Border Khmer: A Demographic Study of the Residents of Site 2, Site B, and Site 8," November 1989. www.websitesrcg.com/border/documents/survey-1989.html.

5. Roger Normand, Human Rights Program, Harvard Law School, "Refugee Voices: Inside Site Two," *Journal of Refugee Studies*, 3, no. 2 (1990).

Chapter Fourteen

A BARBED-WIRE EMBRACE

Family Reunions

Behold, I have set before you an open door,
which no one is able to shut.

—Revelation 3:8

Though like the wanderer, the sun gone down,
darkness be over me, my rest a stone;
yet in my dreams I'd be nearer, my God, to thee;
nearer, my God, to thee, nearer to thee!

—Sara F. Adams

THE BEST illusions are created with a fraction of reality mixed in. So to be able to act as if I was planning to stay in Cambodia, I had to do just that, at least for a while. During my last days in Laem Son, I pretended I would stay forever. It took every ounce of my patience to pull that off. The hardest investment in the ruse was time. Especially when every bone in my body was ready to flee.

Before my friend Mee left me in Laem Son, which is known as the Pine Headland, I met my sister-in-law and her new husband, Jai, the village head. This was to be my last stop before what I hoped would be freedom and safety. Jai suggested that I stay a long time and do all I could to quell any suspicion. I was a newcomer to the village, but when I lingered and even began to cut down trees and collect palm leaves—enough to build a large house—the villagers and officers began to trust me. Then Kanika and Sokunaroat arrived. And soon after them, Boury and Shalom.

I supported us by fishing, and in the process garnered more credibility with the locals. The sea was a formidable workplace, and the pay—75 Thai *Baht* ($3 US) per day—wasn't much, but it kept us from imposing on Jai and his family. Boury used her nursing skills, and villagers soon sought out her assistance. A friend in Sihanoukville, who worked in a pharmacy, sent medicine to Boury by way of the fishermen.

One day Jai introduced me to his younger brother

Yen, who owned a pretty large fishing boat, so I disclosed to him our desire to go to Thailand.

"I can arrange your escape," he said. "Don't worry! But you must not travel in a large group in my boat. I'll take you first, along with only one or maybe two of your daughters. Then the others can follow."

What Yen said was encouraging, but it almost didn't seem real. Again we had to plan our strategy as a family. And again we could not travel together. I decided to take Shalom and Kanika with me. Sokunaroat would come with Boury because she was strong and didn't suffer from seasickness like Shalom and Kanika did. I was, by now, a seasoned sailor and knew I could look after Shalom and Kanika.

Yen and I traveled with Shalom and Kanika to Khlong Yai, where he and his Thai wife, Dam, had a house. Shalom was only four years old and acclimated immediately to her new surroundings. She even began to forget Khmer as she practiced Thai with her new friends every day. Soon after the three of us arrived, Boury and Sokunaroat joined us.

I knew we would need to travel farther inland to be safe. And I wasn't yet convinced that a refugee camp was our only option. This was just before the 1985 UN agreement with the Thai government that no Cambodians would be allowed to live in Thailand outside the camps. I asked Dam to find a way for me to travel west and farther inland to visit the Trat municipality. She discouraged the idea.

"Do you have any relatives there? You know, the cost of living is very high and you don't have any money."

"Dam, I am a Christian," I said. "I have a hundredfold brothers and a hundredfold sisters all over the world. I know there is a church in Trat. Deliver the letter I'm going to write, please. You can take it to the pastor or any of the elders there."

She looked skeptical.

"Just take the letter. You'll see."

I wrote my letter to Dr. Preeda, a medical doctor I knew about, who was an elder of the church in Trat. Dam went to his clinic and took a number in order to be seen as a patient. When her time came and Dr. Preeda asked her what he could do for her, she handed him my letter. He read it out loud.

"Where is my brother Barnabas?" he asked.

"He's at my house, about 74 kilometers from here."

Dam was amazed at what Dr. Preeda did next.

With a quick, "Follow me," he strode into the waiting room of his clinic and announced, "I am so sorry, but the clinic is closing for the rest of the day. I have a family affair that I must deal with right away. Please come to see me tomorrow."

How better to demonstrate to Dam that the church is a family?

I was praying on the beach in Khlong Yai when the two of them approached. From a distance I knew who it was and ran to meet them. As Dr. Preeda and I embraced like long-lost brothers, I thought of Jesus' words in Matthew 19:29–30 (GNT): "Everyone who has left houses or brothers or sisters or father or mother or children or fields for my sake, will receive a hundred times more and will be given eternal life."

Dr. Preeda promised to solicit help and prayer from the church in Trat. Not only that, he contacted his pastor, Sa-ngob, and missionaries in neighboring provinces to enlist their advice and help. Before he returned home, Dam agreed to take me on the dangerous journey inland to Trat. Because there were checkpoints along the way, we decided I should make the trip first. Sokunaroat and Kanika would come next. Finally, Boury and Shalom.

Dam and I took a taxi and headed west. I, of course, had no ID and no official Thai documentation. As we approached the first checkpoint, where I would be required to show identification to the border patrol, I prayed out loud, "Lord, I don't have an ID to show these men. You know what my family needs."

We stopped behind a line of cars and I continued to pray. Just as the car in front pulled away from the checkpoint, it began to rain—hard—and the guard simply waved us on!

Before we reached Trat, we had to stop at another

checkpoint and wait behind another line of cars. Dam asked, "What are you going to do this time?"

"I am going to pray for another miracle."

"Are you going to pray for rain again?" Dam laughed.

"No," I said. An idea began to form in my mind. "It won't rain this time. This time I am going to sleep."

The taxi pulled up to the checkpoint, and Dam handed her ID to the guard. "Who's this guy?" he asked, pointing at me.

I pretended to be asleep and heard Dam say, "That's my relative, and he's not feeling well."

"Okay, then. Go."

On the Way to Site II

During those first days I was in Trat, the United Nations signed the agreement that sealed our family's fate. Our only legal option, if we were to live in Thailand, was to go to the shelter of a refugee camp. I decided to stay in Trat with my new church family while waiting for our family to gather. Dam returned to Khlong Yai, where she would send Kanika and Sokunaroat to me. Boury and Shalom would wait with her until it was safe for them to join us.

I used the time to work on my command of the Thai language. I also learned another useful skill: car repair. Pastor Sa-ngob operated a shop that repaired cars for the entire community. Some of these belonged to police officers. These men knew I was Cambodian, but never seemed bothered by the fact. One even looked me in the eye one day and said, "Good luck with your family reunion."

Finally the day came for Kanika and Sokunaroat to arrive in Trat. They were to come straight to the church in the early afternoon following the Sunday morning service. That morning I shared communion with the church members and then, that afternoon, we had lunch—delicious chicken curry—together.

I had never seen a congregation fellowship together in this way before. It was a lovely experience . . . until the afternoon stretched on and on and Kanika and Sokunaroat did not arrive. While the others continued to eat and talk and laugh, I knelt in a corner and prayed. Through my tears, I asked God to protect my girls from the dangers I knew were all too common. They could have been caught in a skirmish and shot. They could have been raped and left for dead by their guide. They could have been arrested. In those years the Thai border was notorious for corruption and violence. Why had I allowed them to travel alone? Where were they?

"Barnabas! Your daughters are here!"

I jumped up to greet them and, I'm embarrassed to say, I didn't even let them eat until they told us why they were so late.

Just as I had done the month before, they at first rode

in a taxi. But eventually their guide got them out of the car and led them a long way into the forest. He explained they had to walk to avoid the checkpoints, but the longer they walked, the more frightened they became. They began to worry the guide had plans to attack them where no one would hear them cry for help. Eventually the trees cleared and they saw a small house in a grove. He took them to the door and introduced them to the old man who lived there. They knew enough Thai to understand what the old man said to their guide: "Are you planning to harm these two girls?"

"No, no, uncle, I would never do such a thing. I promised their mother I would deliver them safely to their father in Trat."

And that's exactly what the faithful guide did. He was still with the girls when they arrived, so I thanked him. I told him I didn't have any money to pay him. He explained that he owed Yen and Dam, and helping our family was a way to repay them. Besides, he said, "These days we need to share one another's burdens."

In a time when corruption was so widespread and harboring illegal aliens was a severely punishable crime, this man was a rarity. He promised to go back to Khlong Yai and get Boury and Shalom. Meanwhile, the three of us stayed with Pastor Sa-ngob. I worked in the repair shop, and the girls helped with the laundry and cooking for the men who worked with Pastor Sa-ngob.

Boury and Shalom

Pastor Sa-ngob contacted a mentor of his—Reverend Dan Cobb of Chanthaburi Baptist Church—and asked him to help secure Thai citizenship for my family. If we became citizens, I thought, we could stay closer to our country, our people, and our culture. Using every possible channel of communication and any available legal means, Dan contacted the local Thai authorities and military officers on our behalf. I eagerly awaited the results of his hard work. The news I wanted to hear next was that Boury and Shalom were on the way to Trat, but instead I heard some very bad news.

Every year the Thais celebrate their king's birthday. It is a solemn occasion that begins at 8:00 a.m. when everyone, wherever they are, salutes the flag. On this particular day—which Boury did not know had any special meaning—Boury went to the open market in Khlong Yai to buy milk and medicine. She was intent on her task and didn't notice that everyone stopped to salute the flag, nor did she stop to pay her respects.

On any other day, Boury blended in. But on this day, without meaning to, she may as well have announced that she was a foreigner. An officer called and told her to stop. But she did not understand Thai and didn't know he was speaking to her. Enraged, the officer followed and arrested her. When I got word of her arrest, she was still in the police station at Khlong Yai with no real hope of a release.

Shalom was distraught, as would any four-year-old whose mother and father are both absent.

My heart was broken. I determined to go back to get Boury and Shalom myself. I assumed I would be arrested as well, but at least I would be with Boury and share her fate. At least, I hoped, I could check on Shalom and make sure she was in good hands. I asked the church in Trat to pray. I also asked Pastor Sa-ngob to take charge of my two daughters.

"Would you consider Kanika and Sokunaroat your foster daughters?"

"Yes, of course."

"If you find any suitable young men for them, would you arrange their weddings?"

"I'll do my best."

I loved Boury and Shalom so much that I did not feel like eating. So I fasted and prayed for three days before I left. One day, as I stood outside and watched the sunset, I was reminded of the Cambodian horizon. I told the Lord I was confused, but even though I didn't know what horizon I would see in the future, I knew my destiny was in Him. I asked Him to lead me.

I immediately sensed that I should write my friend Andrew Way, one of the first OMF missionaries I met in Phnom Penh in the early '70s. He sent back a letter of encouragement with Romans 1:1: "Paul, a servant of Christ Jesus, called to be an apostle and set apart for the gospel of God" (NIV). Now I was even more confused. I wasn't sure what the verse meant for me.

Andrew contacted another friend of ours, Professor Sathapon, from Khon Kaen University in Thailand, and asked him to advise me. In mid-1974, Sathapon had visited Andrew in Cambodia. At the time I was staying with Andrew at the Youth Center near the Olympic stadium in Phnom Penh. Sathapon met me and became my first Thai friend—and I his first Cambodian one. While waiting to hear from Professor Sathapon, Sokunaroat offered to work as a maid for a Thai family to earn enough bribe money to free her mother. Most police officers could be "bought" for around 10,000 Baht, or about 400 US dollars. If both girls worked, they could raise the funds fairly quickly.

"Are you kidding me?
Your wife is in jail and your
youngest daughter is living among
strangers. And you want me
to pray for a recording studio?"

Professor Sathapon traveled by bus from Khon Kaen to Trat, nearly seven hundred kilometers, to meet me and encourage me to pray and wait for a better way. Bribe money would most likely not solve things permanently. Boury would just be rearrested, and more money would be required. It was a circuitous system and we could not hope to beat it. We continued to pray for a "better way." As we prayed, the Lord led me in a strange direction.

The church in Trat communicated regularly with a British missionary in Bangkok named Ali Blair. She later became the liaison between me and the fledgling church in the refugee camp. She contacted me to ask how she could pray for me and my family. I asked her if she would pray for one thing: a recording studio.

"Are you kidding me?" Ali responded. "Your wife is in jail and your youngest daughter is living as a stranger among strangers. Your teenage daughters are seriously considering selling themselves to earn bribe money. And you want me to pray for a *recording studio*?"

"We are approaching the throne of God, the King of grace," I said. "I want to make a big deal with our big God. I just wrote a song based on Psalm 27:4: 'I have asked the Lord for one thing; one thing only do I want: to live in the Lord's house all my life, to marvel there at his goodness, and to ask for his guidance' [GNT]. These verses confirm to me not only that God has called me to be a songwriter and worship leader—a calling I cannot deny—but they also encourage me to ask for only one thing, and to choose that one thing wisely."

I'm not sure Ali was with me, so I hurried to finish: "How can I possibly fulfill this calling to write songs and lead people in worship unless I have a recording studio? And how can I run a recording studio without my wife cooking for us? How can I make music unless my daughters sing with me? This one request covers everything."

Ali Blair agreed, though I wonder how enthusiastically. I'm certain, like me, she couldn't wait to see how God would handle this request. Surely an adventure was under way.

The next Sunday a friend and brother in the Lord visited me at Trat Christian Church. He was about to be married, and I expected him to direct our conversation toward his beautiful fiancée and their upcoming wedding. Instead, he brought a gift and an unusual explanation: "As you know, weddings and receptions cost money." My friend smiled. "I had just exactly enough saved to cover the costs, but the Lord placed it on my heart to spend the money differently. I didn't understand why, but God led me to buy the best sound equipment I could find for you. I don't know if you can use it."

I was too stunned to comment.

"I purchased a set of portable studio equipment and some musical instruments in Singapore," my friend said, "and brought them with me. I know it doesn't make sense, but I felt I had to simply obey the leadership of the Holy Spirit. My only request is that you look after the equipment and use it for the sake of the gospel."

Now we knew beyond any shadow of a doubt that a bribe was not the way to proceed. I took my Cambodian hymnbook and flute and set off in a taxi for Khlong Yai. I felt excited. What crazy thing would God do next? I wondered what miracle He would use this time to get me past the checkpoints. With a renewed confidence in the Lord and in the advisability of doing things His way, I decided I would simply answer with the truth to anyone who stopped me.

At the first checkpoint, when they asked me for my ID, I smiled and said, "I don't have one because I am a Cambodian citizen."

"Why are you smiling?" the guard asked. "Are you on something?"

"I am smiling," I said, "because the Lord answered my prayer."

"Who is your Lord?"

"Jesus is my Lord."

"And what is your prayer?"

"My prayer is this: I asked the Lord to take me straight to my wife who is now being held in the police station at Khlong Yai. I know the Lord answered me because you can send me to her, and today I will see her."

"You're wrong," the guard said. "We would never knowingly send a husband to the same police station as his wife. We keep families separate."

I couldn't stop smiling. "You would never do that."

"How do you know I would never do that?"

"Because you are the Thai people. You're nice people. Your king is known all over the world as the nicest king of all. That's why the UN decided to work with the Thai government to set up refugee camps. You would never ruin the reputation of your king and queen."

I could tell the guard was confused. He changed the subject. "What do you do back home in Cambodia?"

"I am a musician."

The guard was clearly interested, so I offered to prove it by playing a tune for him. He walked me back to the taxi to get my flute and two hymnbooks, one in Khmer and the other in Thai. When he looked at the hymnbooks, he saw the word "Jesus" in Thai and asked me, point-blank, "Are you a Christian?"

"Yes, I am."

At this point the guards let the taxi driver go. I could tell he was relieved. Although he knew nothing of my story—which is why the guards released him—it wasn't safe to do business with Christians.

When we were back in the interrogation room, I breathed a silent prayer, brought my flute to my lips, and played *Nearer My God to Thee*. I couldn't help it; the tears began to flow. They ran down my cheeks and onto my bare chest. (My shirt had been removed at the beginning of my questioning so the guards could check for evidence of drug use.) I abruptly ended the song and looked up.

Several of the guards had gathered to listen, and they also were weeping. "Please play another tune for us. We are so far away from the city out here and we never hear any music."

Next, I played *Jesus, Savior, Pilot Me.* That hymn told my story. I had been in a stormy sea, unsure where to go, and Jesus piloted me safely to shore.

> Jesus, Savior, pilot me,
> Over life's tempestuous sea;
> Unknown waves before me roll,
> Hiding rock and treach'rous shoal;
> Chart and compass came from Thee:
> Jesus, Savior, pilot me.
>
> As a mother stills her child,
> Thou canst hush the ocean wild;
> Boist'rous waves obey Thy will
> When Thou say'st to them, "Be still!"
> Wondrous Sov'reign of the sea,
> Jesus, Savior, pilot me.
>
> When at last I near the shore,
> And the fearful breakers roar
> 'Twixt me and the peaceful rest,
> Then, while leaning on Thy breast,

> May I hear Thee say to me,
> "Fear not, I will pilot thee."

The guard begged me to play one more song, so I played a Khmer tune I had recently written with gospel lyrics. "That's a Thai song! That's a Thai song!" the men said.

"No, it's Khmer," I said. "Our cultures share many commonalities, especially in our musical forms."

Next, the chief officer asked if I had any money on me. I assumed this was his prelude to asking for a bribe, but I answered honestly anyway: "I have 500 *baht*."

He asked if he could borrow the money and sent his guards out to buy cakes, candies, and something to drink. As soon as they left he said, "I wanted to have a private chat with you. I wish you had come three months ago," he said. "Then you could have become a Thai citizen. It is time for men like you to suffer no longer. You are so talented. And you're harmless! Thailand needs citizens like you."

"Sir," I said, "I am a nationalist. I know you are too. Have you ever considered leaving Thailand?"

"Oh no!" he said. "I love my nation. I love my people and my culture."

"It's the same with me. I didn't leave Cambodia until the last minute, and only when there were no other alternatives.

"Have you ever heard the parable of the shrimp?" I said. "The shrimp lives contentedly in a warm lake. It never dreams of leaving. But then the lake evaporates and becomes too shallow and too hot for the shrimp. Then the shrimp has to swim away to another lake where the water is deep and warm."

I could tell the guard understood my meaning, but I explained anyway. "I am swimming out of a hot lake. I am looking for a lake with warm water where I can live. Cambodia's temperature rose until, at the last minute, I could no longer live there."

The officer nodded. "What can I do to help?"

"Release me, so I can go to Khlong Yai and find my daughter. I trust my Lord will lead me step-by-step the rest of the way."

He readily agreed and called for a taxi. Meanwhile, the other guards returned with the food and 470 *baht* in change. An hour before, when I handed over my last 500 *baht*, I assumed I would never get it back. This was icing on the cake, a simple reminder that God was just and good and merciful.

Barely Room to Leap for Joy

I went straight to Yen and Dam's home and found Shalom. She cried when she saw me, and I wept and turned my face away. "Lord," I cried out, "look on this little one who misses her mother so much. Please be quick to reunite us with her mother!"

The next morning, as Shalom and I sat playing together on the floor, the landlord burst through the door and announced that a police officer was on his way to inspect the house. If he found us, things would be even worse for Boury. It was bad enough that she was an illegal alien, but harboring other Cambodians in her home would add more severe charges.

The landlord opened the doors to a wooden cabinet and shoved both Shalom and me inside. Shalom was perfectly obedient and stayed silent, even when we heard the police officer and the landlord arguing.

"Where is Mr. Barnabas?" the officer yelled.

"He is not here."

"If he loves his wife and child as much as she says he does, he would be here. He wouldn't have run away."

"You're right about the first part; he didn't run away," the landlord said, "but he is not here right now."

The officer left, but only for a moment. Shalom wanted to know why we were still hiding, so the two of us began to pray, in part just to keep her occupied. The police officer returned and again harangued the poor landlord. Finally, he left and the landlord whispered that he thought it was safe to unlock the cabinet and let us out.

Just as the key slid into the lock, we heard the officer return a third time. I froze, assuming this was it. There was no way the two of us could stay hidden any longer.

"Darling, don't be afraid! I'm here. You can come out."

It was Boury! I was so surprised and delighted, I leaped for joy as the landlord opened the door to let us out. Forgetting the cramped quarters I'd been in for the past hour, I hit my head on the low ceiling of the cabinet. Everyone in the room laughed, and the tension of the past few days melted away.

It turns out that Ali Blair had sent a report to the UNHCR of our family's plight. Also, the church had petitioned the government asking for Boury's release. That very morning three UNHCR (United Nations High Commissioner for Refugees) officials from Chanthaburi visited Boury in jail. Once they secured her release, they accompanied her to find Shalom and me. They assured the landlord he would not be prosecuted for hiding us. They also questioned us thoroughly about Kanika and Sokunaroat so they could trace their location in Trat and bring us all together. Shalom wept again to see her mother, but this time she shed tears of joy.

In a Holding Pattern

It was October 1985. We were finally all together in Kamput Holding Center, a staging post—more like a prison—in Chanthaburi, next to the Cambodian border. It was cold, and we could hear shelling nearby, but we were together.

At first, we almost didn't make it. First, Kanika and Sokunaroat were determined to haul the studio equipment and instruments from Trat. I urged them to leave it all behind, but they insisted. They understood, perhaps better than I did in the middle of the crisis, how important this equipment would be in the future. And they were right. Eventually, we had to leave some of it. They chose a portable Boss BX-800 eight-channel stereo mixer, two Sony electret condenser stereo microphones, and a professional Sony TC-D5M analog tape recorder.

The recording equipment caused the officers who processed our forms to wonder if I was a KGB or CIA agent. I had to explain very carefully that the purpose of this equipment was solely to create Christian music. Thankfully, they believed me.

Next we were transferred to the prison in Khao I Dang Holding Center in Prachinburi, where we stayed for a month. Most people traveled light to the camps, so the security officer at Khao I Dang questioned the wisdom of carrying the heavy sound equipment. This caused me to reflect on the fact that God's answers to our prayers can at times prove irksome. But my prayer for a recording studio wasn't just a trick to get my family back; it was a request that took the work of the kingdom into account.

Once again, we were in prison. The buildings, encircled with barbed wire and topped with corrugated tin roofs, were home to Muslims, Buddhists, and some Cambodians who had committed offenses against the Thai people or the Thai authority. Again, it was quite cold.

A teacher of English in Khao I Dang Holding Center sent us a personal letter:

> You taught me English in Cambodia when I was just a peasant boy and had no money to pay you. When I left Phnom Penh, I ended up in Khao I Dang Camp where I teach English to make money. I am basically in hiding, so I cannot visit you, but I can send my Christian brother to you with this gift of fried chicken.

We decided to share the food with our new Buddhist and Muslim friends. I asked, "Who will say grace?"

"You," they all but shouted. "Because God has shown His grace through you, we want you to say grace."

This scene—people of three faiths sharing a meal delivered by Christian friends—repeated itself over and over during our month at the prison in Khao I Dang. Two young soldiers decided to believe in Jesus after Boury shared the gospel with them. I counseled them and other new believers. Boury got into the habit of throwing bananas and packets of instant noodles to the soldiers who had been arrested and were imprisoned there in a room separated from ours by a barbed-wire wall.

Another Clinic Closes for the Day
and Another Door Opens

While we were at the prison in Khao I Dang, Kanika woke in the middle of the night with a severe toothache. A dentist volunteered her time at the camp, and we arranged for Kanika to see her as soon as possible. Before treating her, the dentist looked over the information on the form Kanika had filled out. She looked up from the paperwork with a big smile.

"Is your father *Lokrou* Barnabas the songwriter?

"Yes, that's my dad."

"The Lord brought you here, Kanika," the dentist said. "I am a Christian too."

He greeted me heartily
from his side of the barbed wire,
then reached out to embrace me.
We hugged with our arms
through the fence, hardly heeding
the barrier between us.

As soon as she treated Kanika's toothache—with utmost professional care—she walked into the waiting room and informed everyone the clinic was now closed for the day. She went immediately to her church to tell them the family they had been praying for for two months was at the prison. Then she went from church to church telling them God had answered their prayers, and our family was here. That day fifty Cambodian brothers and sisters in Christ walked to the camp to greet us.

Pastor Mak Chhouk, the dentist's pastor, had followed our journey since the days we first left Phnom Penh. At each step along the way, I received letters of encouragement from him, so finally meeting him in person was pure joy. He was a huge bear of a man. He greeted me heartily from his side of the barbed wire, then reached out to embrace me. We hugged with our arms through the fence and then stood, hardly heeding the barrier between us, talking as if we had known each other for years.

"Dad, you're bleeding!" Sokunaroat said, pointing at the blood on my shirt where the barbs had pressed into my chest. Pastor Chhouk had the same red stains on his shirt. Neither of us cared.

Visits were not allowed in the center, because it doubled as a prison, except across the fence—and even then, for only fifteen minutes. But I should have known by then that God can open any door if He so chooses. The Thai commandant announced to the other men, "This is truly a unique family. Their documentation is in order, and we can trust them. Let them talk as long as they want. Open the prison doors and let the visitors come on in."

All fifty visitors, including the dentist, poured into the camp. They brought fruit and fried chicken and stayed long enough for us to feel, by the time they left, as if we had just experienced our best party and family celebration ever. I couldn't help but think of the passage our family had read that very morning in our devotional time together:

> I know your works. Behold, I have set before you an open door, which no one is able to shut. I know that you have but little power, and yet you have kept my word and have not denied my name. (Revelation 3:8)

From then on, for the entire time we stayed in Khao I Dang, visitors came and went through the door God opened. "I'm here to see *Lokrou* Barnabas," was all they had to say, and the guards let them in. God had indeed set before us an open door.

Chapter Fifteen

THE VALUE SYSTEM
OF THE KINGDOM

Inside Out and Upside Down

For he who is least among you all
is the one who is great.

—Jesus (Luke 9:48)

The biggest disease today is not leprosy . . .
but rather the feeling of being unwanted.

—Mother Teresa of Calcutta

Shallow understanding from people of good will
is more frustrating than absolute misunderstanding
from people of ill will. Lukewarm acceptance
is much more bewildering than outright rejection.

—Martin Luther King Jr.

A CAMBODIAN proverb goes something like this: "The rich are to care for the poor as the garment does the body. The wise are to care for the foolish as the ship does the small boats that float in its wake." By the time we reached Site II in Thailand, I had lived long enough to see this maxim turned on its head by my country's leaders.

Torn garments and sunken ships; that's about all the poor and the foolish could expect from their leaders. But I served a King who stooped low to serve His people. I served a Master who willingly became a slave and expected His followers to do the same. I served a Leader who placed the highest value on "the least." Site II was where I would learn what this really meant.

An Open Door

The political landscape between our two countries was quite complicated, and the refugee camps throughout Thailand were controlled by a confusing mix of parties or factions. The UNHCR (United Nations High Commissioner for Refugees) supported Khao I Dang, our final stop before Site II. Khao I Dang was a camp for refugees who were awaiting migration to the United States, Australia, Canada, or elsewhere. In Khao I Dang camp, men were not expected to join the military because they were on their way to another country. All the refugees in the camp, including the men, were given food rations.

The UNBRO (United Nations Border Relief Operation)

supported Site B, Site 8, Site II, and a few other small
camps. The FUNCINPEC, the royalist political party,
maintained a camp, Site B in Surin. Another border camp,
Site 8 in Prachinburi was run by the PDK (the Khmer
Rouge Party of Democratic Kampuchea). Site II in Prach-
inburi was run by the KPLNF (Khmer People's National
Liberation Front), a minority army that fought against the
Vietnamese in Cambodia.

Almost every day, soldiers left Site II to fight just across
the border. All of us who were supported by UNBRO were
considered displaced persons. Men and boys did not receive food rations at all. UNBRO agreed not to give us food
rations because many of us joined the resistance army to
fight the Cambodian Vietnamese allied army. The way
they figured it, we couldn't fight if we were hungry.

Boury, the girls, and I spent our first week in the new
arrival section of Site II. Again the studio equipment gave
the guards reason to suspect that I was a spy, but one of
the Japanese UN officials, who it turned out was a Christian, vouched for us, and the equipment made it through
yet another time.

Our arrival at this particular camp was significant.
It symbolized our commitment to Cambodia—a commitment God had been steering us slowly toward over the
past eleven months during our exodus from Phnom Penh
to Thailand. While I was in Trat and Boury was in Khlong
Yai, we still entertained the notion that we might escape

to the United States. It made sense. Boury had two cousins there. I had connections with World Vision International. It seemed a wise option to consider.

After the UNHCR officials released Boury from the prison in Khlong Yai and reunited us, I met with them, and they asked me if we were interested in going to America. They would begin the paperwork to send us there. I just needed to say the word. But I told them no, we wanted to stay as close as we could to our own people and our own culture. That night I asked Boury if I had made a mistake. In refusing their offer, I had closed the door to the United States.

"No," she said, "it must be from the Lord."

We would stay in Thailand until
we could repatriate to Cambodia.
There was no way to know
it would be eight years.

So our fate was sealed. We would stay in Thailand until we could repatriate to Cambodia. There was no way to know it would be eight years before we could go home.

Recently I reflected on what this restriction—we were basically imprisoned for the next eight years—would one day produce. In February 2011, I traveled two and a half hours from Phnom Penh to Kampot Province, where I preached on Romans 6 in a message titled "Sin shall not have dominion over you." Close to one thousand people from the surrounding rural areas gathered to listen. At the end of the day, local pastors from thirty-eight brand-new house churches baptized 715 Cambodians in the shallow waters of Romlich Lake.

These pastors were trained and mentored by thirteen church planters who began their kingdom work through Ambassadors for Christ International (AFCI) Cambodia in 1998. These men have so far planted eighty-one house churches.

Had we escaped to the United States, I would have most likely become the pastor of a small Cambodian church in an American city. Our family would have planted one seed in the ground. It would have grown, but because it wasn't *our* soil—not our native land and not the ground God intended for us to farm—I wonder if the church's growth might have suffered.

Although we had our share of ups and downs during our eight-year stay in Thailand, I became more and more certain that the open door God had unlocked for us was a Cambodian door. The intervening years seem to bear this out.

When we finally left Site II for our homeland in March 1993, we packed quite differently from the way we had eight years previously. Boury wanted to take the church curtains (we did) and all the dishes (we took those too) she had used the past few Christmases when she cooked chicken curry for five hundred church members.

The refugee church was thriving. In eight years it had produced a bumper crop of young pastors, a network of fiery leaders who have since invaded our country with the gospel, so that now, including the new house churches, there are upwards of four hundred churches where in 1985 there had been only three.

New Friendships with an Old Acquaintance and an Old Enemy

Our very first day at Site II was eventful in several ways. We were still filling out paperwork when a Jeep pulled up to the arrival center and three important men stepped out. Only VIPs rode in Jeeps. The US Secretary of State, George Schultz, walked to the crude building where we sat waiting for our final processing. He was flanked on one side by an attaché from the US embassy in Bangkok, a man named Kem Sos, who had spent the years of Lon Nol's administration studying in the United States. During the years of the Killing Fields, he had worked in the United States. At his other side strode a KPNLF general who asked if anyone spoke English and would translate for them during their visit. I volunteered. I was the only English speaker in the center that day.

The general asked me a series of questions in rapid succession. Where was I born? What high school did I attend? And so on. Then he asked, "Who was the governor of your province during Lon Nol's regime?"

I grinned at him and said, "You."

General Dien Del was pleased that I remembered him. How could I not? Before the Khmer Rouge took over, I had been the president of my high school alumni association when he was governor of Kandal Province, and we had met many times. General Del was instrumental in helping me procure books for the high school's library.

I translated for the three men during their visit that day, and just as they were preparing to leave, General Del reached into his pockets and pulled out every *baht* he could find—about two thousand—and handed them to me. He then said to the guards at the new arrival center, "Take good care of this man."

It had not been that many years since "take care of him" were the Khmer Rouge's code words for execution. God was slowly beginning to redeem the very words of the Killing Fields. The money General Del shared with us that day, almost as an afterthought, provided enough food to sustain our family for the next several months.

That same night I noticed a man with light skin sitting alone and looking more dejected than any of the other refugees. I could tell he was Vietnamese. I could also sense the Holy Spirit nudging me to engage him in conversation. Not only did I know I should greet him in a friendly way, I knew I would not be at peace until I shared with him the good news of the gospel.

"But Lord," I argued internally, "he is my enemy. The Vietnamese are the very reason I had to leave Cambodia. Surely You don't expect me to even look at him, much less talk to him."

Though Pol Pot, a native Cambodian, had wreaked so much havoc in our country and on our people in the past years, the grudge we felt as a nation against the Vietnamese ran deeper, and we had nursed it longer. If not for them, Pol Pot may not have succeeded. If not for the Vietnamese, whose army now exploded their shells in our fields just across the border, we might be safe and at home.

The Vietnamese were the sole reason an unholy triumvirate of factions now coexisted, and fought to free Cambodia of the very army that had liberated us from the iron fist of the Khmer Rouge. (An alliance of the FUNC-INPEC [the Royalist Party], the KPNLF, and the PDK [the Khmer Rouge, or the Party of Democratic Kampuchea] eventually became known as the Coalition Government of Democratic Kampuchea [CGDK].)

I wrestled with my feelings, feelings as imbedded in my DNA as the color of my skin. But I was a new man, wasn't I? I had a new DNA, a new internal code—and that code reminded me that I was to love my enemies. Jesus did not hate His enemies, He loved them. He didn't just tolerate them, He loved them. How could I not do the same?

Hien, my "enemy" and new friend from Vietnam, accepted Christ that night, which is rather miraculous given his circumstances. He had been a Vietnamese military officer working in Cambodia before escaping to Thailand. When his wife arrived before he did at Site II, she claimed she did not have a husband—though she was pregnant at the time with his child. Because the camp was run by the KPNLF, she felt that disclosing her marriage to a Vietnamese military officer would endanger both of them. This ruse worked in her favor. She was able to leave with Hien's son and go to Canada.

But her lie had dismal consequences for Hien. No one believed they were married. He begged for an opportunity to reunite with her in Canada, to no avail. He was a man of action, and a desperate one at that. He went to the Khmer Intelligence Security Agency (KISA) and offered to share secret military information in exchange for the freedom to join his wife in Canada. The men at the KISA office agreed to Hien's proposal. After he had spilled every piece of pertinent information, they helped him complete an application form for his family reunion and sent it to the Canadian embassy in Bangkok. But Hien's case was rejected. His account contradicted his wife's claims.

Next, he spent a lot of money on illegal guides who took him first to Singapore and then to Malaysia—again with no results except that all his money was gone. He had tried everything. He showed me a letter from his wife in which she begged him not to pursue illegal means to get to Canada. By the time I met him, he felt not only defeated but also ashamed that he had stooped so low in his endeavor to reunite with his wife and son.

Coming to Christ, at the core, involves leaving human effort behind. We must not only realize that our human attempts to gain salvation are woefully ineffective, we must also admit that our efforts to control our very *lives* are equally ineffective. When Hien gave his life to Christ, he gave the Lord this sticky situation. The quest to join his family had become his life, his obsession, so he gave it up and offered it to the Lord. I explained to him that human effort was never satisfying. The only answer was surrender.

We stayed in the new arrival center for another week. During that time I poured into Hien as much truth and encouragement as I could. He received it like a dry sponge soaks up water. He spoke impeccable Khmer, so communicating with each other was no problem.

Nothing about his separation from his wife and son changed, but he began to be at peace. Then we went our separate ways: Boury, the girls, and I to one section of Site II, and Hien to *Trai Moi*, or "new camp," an area specifically built for the Vietnamese. I knew the pastor of the *Tinh Lan*[1] church there, and I introduced the two of them.

We had no trouble visiting one another for the first few years, and Hien became my close friend.

Two years later, every one of the Vietnamese pastors in *Trai Moi* was relocated to America, leaving that section of the camp without a pastor. Hien began to fill the missing leadership roles, along with some others who were left behind. He asked me then if I would help him contact the Canadian embassy in Bangkok. Although I loved Hien, I initially found it hard to trust him. It wasn't his fault. My old feelings about the Vietnamese took a long time to change. By now I was convinced he was a sincere man, so I agreed to help.

I wrote the letter to the embassy. In it I commented that it didn't make sense for a Cambodian to advocate for a Vietnamese. Surely the authorities could deduce that I was sincere in vouching for this man. I collected photographs of Hien and his wife when they were dating, engaged, and at their wedding, and sent them as proof that he was indeed the husband of his wife and the father of his child. And then we waited. And waited.

In the meantime *Trai Moi* closed, and Hien was sent to a more remote camp called *Ban Thad.* I had made several influential friends in the Catholic church through my friend Daniel from Phnom Penh, who was now at Site II. (Daniel was my friend at the Samaki Hotel who delivered my letters during the underground church days.) A good friend, Father Alfonso de Juan, acquired travel documents for us so Hien and I could continue to visit each other.

I discovered that his Christian friends in *Ban Thad* were encouraging him to leave for Australia. On my next visit Hien met me with some good news: he had just gained approval to go to Australia. Once there, he could more easily work toward getting to Canada. I patted him on the back, genuinely glad for him, and said, "That's good news! Keep praying. The best is yet to come!"

I'm not sure why I said that, but I was right. The next week Hien met me with even better news from the embassy in Bangkok: he was going to Canada! He is still a leader in a Vietnamese church in Canada.

Touching the Untouchables

The English class I had begun to teach dwindled from fifteen students to only two. I am not the most sensitive man, but I noticed people were avoiding me. I was pretty sure I knew why. It all began with an answer to prayer.

We lived in section 5 (also called Commune 5). We had already met a number of Christians who gathered with us for worship. It seemed to me as if we were a tiny speck of light that was almost swallowed up in darkness. The actual darkness was so dangerous it was overwhelming. Outside our door at night the fighting continued, both over the border and in the dirt roads and alleys that scored the camp. Families were under immense pressure and fought with one another.

I knew the potential for the body of Christ to illuminate its community, but we were small, and the community God had placed us in—section 5—was small as well. One night I prayed, "Lord, shine the light of Your gospel in this place. Transform these people and make this community one of brotherly love." I also asked the Lord to bring new people into our section of Site II.

No answer to prayer
has ever challenged me more,
nor taught me more about
the unconditional love of Christ.

The next day, new houses began to be hastily constructed. New houses meant new neighbors, and those new neighbors came as soon as the houses were ready: lepers, all of them. No answer to prayer has ever challenged me more, nor taught me more about the unconditional love of Christ.

These lepers came from a hospital in Khao I Dang. What I didn't know was that they had all begun treatment, which meant they were no longer contagious. I didn't know anything about the disease back then. But I did know that, just as God prompted me to hurdle my own feelings in order to love Hien, I must love the lepers. Just as I taught the young refugee church, "Love your enemies," I began to teach, "Jesus loves the lepers. We must love them too."

But it wasn't easy. Our new neighbors looked hideous, their skin mottled and discolored, their facial features sunken and distorted, their hands and feet often missing fingers or toes. One evening I became ill and couldn't get out of bed. The news of my sickness spread like a disease throughout section 5.

The next day one of the leper families visited our home, and the man offered to give me a therapeutic massage. How could I say no? Every minute of that massage was torture. I turned my head to the wall and closed my eyes, praying I would not vomit because the smell of rotting flesh was so strong. I asked the Lord to help me be grateful. I didn't want to offend our new friends, but I wasn't sure I could do much more than tolerate them.

There was another reason I struggled to love the lepers. Because I did not know much about the disease, I assumed these people were contagious, so I was eaten up with fear for Shalom. Boury and I went to visit a leper couple who had just had a baby. We took a gift, but we left Shalom at home and hoped they wouldn't wonder why. I was afraid she might be even more susceptible because she was young. Every encounter with our new neighbors sent me into a frenzy of worry for her.

The day after the massage, a young woman doctor visited our section. I noticed that she greeted each leper warmly and gave each of them a hug. She didn't cringe or seem the least afraid to touch them. I invited her to have lunch at our home. After we ate, I asked, "Doctor, is leprosy more contagious to our Shalom because she is so young?"

The doctor laughed and said, "Oh no, they aren't contagious at all . . . Shalom isn't in danger. In fact, no one can 'catch' leprosy from these people."

She went on to explain that these patients had begun treatment and were free of the disease. They were in Site II waiting for plastic surgery "to become beautiful again."

"Oh Lord," I cried after she left, "forgive me for doubting You. Forgive me for refusing to love completely."

After that, I was not afraid. Loyalty was hard to come by in Site II, but the lepers became our loyal friends. One constant concern Boury and I shared was the safety of our adolescent daughters. Young men, including the soldiers who were there to protect us—but who sometimes had nothing better to do than harass and even attack young women—continually loitered in our area.

One afternoon Kanika and a friend decided it would be fun to dress alike. As they walked down the street near our home, a group of soldiers began to taunt them and call them lesbians because they were dressed in similar clothing. Neighbors saw the girls running and stepped between the panicked girls and the armed soldiers. They calmly greeted the soldiers in the Thai language and gave the girls a chance to get away. The soldiers were unnerved by the neighbors and left the area immediately. The neighbors were all lepers.

These men and women and their families became a part of our family. I played football and other popular games with them. The students in my English class noticed. Teaching English had been my livelihood from our first days at Site II, our primary source of income. But a teacher with only two students doesn't make enough money to live. I was out of a job.

Losing my job was a small price to pay for the valuable lesson I had learned. The economy of the kingdom is upside down from any other value system in the world. The weak, the poor, the foolish: these are the most prized possessions in the kingdom. If we are to invest in anyone, it isn't to be in the strong, the rich, or those with the best education. My "enemy" Hien taught me this. My friends the lepers drove it home.

If I wanted to be like Jesus, I would have to go low, not high. Today I am physically strong, well-respected, and resourced. It is my privilege to find "the least" and pour my life into theirs. The lepers—those highly regarded by God—taught me that.

On the Run

These days I live in Phnom Penh, but I travel from time to time to the West. I've noticed something interesting about Western culture: no one stays in one place for very long. It seems to me this is because there are always better options out there. Life in the West is never static.

My life had been the same way—always on the move —but for opposite reasons. I was continually running out of options. During the years of the Killing Fields, there were no options, not even the opportunity to escape. Every move was completely outside my control, calculated by the Khmer Rouge in their relentless push toward the countryside. Later, escape was not optional; it was necessary. Since 1975 I had moved from one place to the next to survive. Running had become second nature to me. But in 1987 I finally got running out of my system.

I had become convinced I needed to escape Site II and return to Khao I Dang. If my family needed safety and security, it sure didn't look like we were going to get it in section 5 of Site II. The KPNLF soldiers were everywhere. The Thai border guards seemed like ineffective puppets. I became obsessed with leaving. So obsessed, I set a plan in motion with very little preparation. Again, a family of five could not travel all at once without arousing suspicion, so I determined to leave with Sokunaroat and Shalom, then send for Boury and Kanika later. That's about the extent of my planning.

The three of us set out late one evening with a hired guide I thought I could trust, though I had no reason to do so. There was no electricity in the camp and only a thin sliver of moonlight that night. The guide led us straight to an opening in the barbed wire where a queue of about twenty refugees stood waiting their turn to be led by Thai soldiers into the open field that would take them to the border.

I hadn't expected this. Nor had I expected to pay yet another fee to get out of the camp. As we stood in line, each waiting to pay a bribe, regret settled over me like a heavy fog. After everyone paid, two armed soldiers led all of us into the field, and two others brought up the rear. I began to talk to the Lord: "I have made a really bad mistake, Lord. I trusted myself to people I didn't know when I should have trusted You. You know me and love me so much. Please forgive me for making such a stupid decision."

I told the Lord what He already knew, that I was walking in complete darkness and didn't have a clue where I was going. It's ironic how clearly I saw this fact out there in that pitch-black field. Why I didn't see it before, in the light of day, I don't know.

It began to grow cold and rainy. Before long our feet left dry land and we were sloshing through a foot of water in the rice paddies. Suddenly gunfire erupted just ahead of us, and people in front of us turned around and began running back toward the camp. We couldn't see anything, but we heard cries of terror and bullets whizzing past our heads. Our young guide whipped around and almost knocked me over as he fled.

I whispered to Sokunaroat to run. Shalom clung to her neck, and we headed as quickly as we could back toward the camp. It was slow going because we didn't want to alert the soldiers to our location by splashing in the shallow water. When the gunfire stopped, about midnight, the rain began.

We eventually reached a large bush in the middle of the rice paddy and decided to hide under it for the night. From the screams and groaning around us—it was almost impossible to tell where the sounds came from—we could tell some of our party had been killed, and others were injured. We had been running for half an hour.

We weren't far from the camp. We listened as refugees called out in agony to their loved ones. Eventually UN ambulances arrived, and aid workers made their way in the dark to the injured. Later, as I reflected that life was fragile and that my hope for any real safety in this world was absurd, we heard a short burst of gunfire from inside Site II, in section 13. Another burglary. We had run *from* danger *into* danger.

In this state of mind I decided to wait until dawn, cautioning the girls to be absolutely silent. We were winded from running, and fear pressed like a fist on our chests. But we held our breath and then released it as slowly and quietly as we could. In the stillness of the last hours before daybreak, we heard a conversation close by. It seemed to be coming from the other side of the bush, *our* bush.

"Where are you headed?" a woman whispered in Khmer.

"I'm looking for a man named Pastor Barnabas," a man said. "My uncle asked me to watch out for him, so I followed the pastor and his two daughters tonight. He entrusted his life to me. But I lost them in the gun battle."

"I'm Barnabas!" I said. "Here we are!"

I reached my right hand through the bush toward the man's voice. He grasped it, and we shook hands in the dark.

As soon as the sun peeked over the eastern mountains, Shalom, Sokunaroat, the man and woman, and I made our way back to the camp. We retrieved two plastic bags with our precious sound equipment that our guide had stashed in the forest. We then slipped back into Site II. Two Thai guards slept soundly in the watchtower. No other guards were in sight. I returned home to a very surprised Boury who told me the entire church had been praying together in our church building throughout the night. My legs were swollen with insect bites and cuts from thorns, and Boury ministered to me. I decided then and there that there would be no more running away. It was settled. Site II was our home.

Note

1. *Tinh Lan* means "good news" and is the name for all Christian and Missionary Alliance churches in Vietnam.

Chapter Sixteen

WHAT LIES BEHIND
THE OPEN DOOR

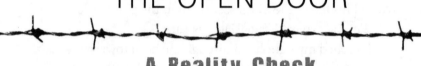

A Reality Check

And pray for us, too, that God may open a door
for our message, so that we may proclaim the
mystery of Christ, for which I am in chains.

—Colossians 4:3 NIV

When one door closes, another opens; but we often
look so long and so regretfully upon the closed door
that we do not see the one which has opened for us.

—Alexander Graham Bell

Shouldn't the existence of even one single refugee
be a cause for alarm throughout the world?

—Urkhan Alakbarov

THERE IS hardly a more imposing image than a closed door. It is an ancient symbol with a universal translation: keep out. Every culture understands the closed door.

A few kilometers north of *Angkor Wat*, King Jayavarman VII built a new capital known as Angkor Thom, or "the great city," toward the end of the twelfth century. The king built his metropolis just a few decades after the death of the mastermind behind *Angkor Wat*, King Suryavarman II. Close to one million people called the great city home until 1431 when the Siamese army invaded, sacked the city, and toppled the Khmer Empire.

Angkor Thom's four walls of sixteen kilometers each were surrounded by a moat with access at five gates. Inside these massive gates were two wooden doors, each seven meters high. If invaders happened to breach the moat, the gate, and the first door, they could be handily trapped between the inner and outer doors. Everything about the five pairs of doors set into the towering gates would have suggested denial to anyone who did not have right of entry.

One can imagine that there were times in the long history of Angkor Thom when these forbidding doors signaled the same message to people inside the gates. Prisoners of the city's rulers or citizens under siege might find the doors equally impenetrable from the inside. A closed door sends a clear message, whether it keeps you in or out.

For my family, the doors slammed shut on everywhere but Site II. We couldn't go home to Cambodia. We couldn't go to the United States or Canada or Australia. We couldn't even go to another camp along the Thai-Cambodian border. Once these doors—all of them—closed with an irrevocable thud, we discovered another kind of door. An open one.

The apostle Paul wrote to the Corinthians during his extended stay in Ephesus: "a wide door for effective work has opened to me" (1 Corinthians 16:9). This open door was probably why Paul stayed longer in Ephesus—a full two years—than any other stop along his missionary journeys. This is the door God opened to us in Site II. And this door—a "door for effective work"—grew wider every day.

First, I got a new job. I became a translator for the School of Fine Arts. Boury and I became good friends with the school's director and his wife. Through these new friends, word spread to people in other countries that we were in Site II, and we began receiving mail from all over. That made us feel far less cut off from the world.

Kanika also found work at the school and eventually became one of the lead vocalists in a group of young singers there. She met a woman through her job and invited her to live with us in our small home. The two men Boury had led to the Lord in Khao I Dang arrived at Site II and moved in with us as well. They helped out quite a bit around the house, primarily hauling water, which was a continual task. But as these two new believers grew in their faith, they also became more and more engaged in kingdom work with us.

> God can and will open doors
> to do His work through us, *and*
> you can expect trouble when
> you walk through those doors.

Next, we moved out of section 5. The Khmer Evangelical Church in section 14 needed a pastor, and they approached me about filling the role. I gladly accepted and our family immediately relocated. Section 14 was much safer and more stable—many of our new neighbors were soldiers who had families. A Sunday school blossomed, and our family made many friends, ones we still treasure. A young man named Borin led our worship. Another man named Vara had beautiful handwriting and offered to use this skill for the kingdom. While we lived in section 14, I dictated to him eight volumes of *The Khmer Picture Bible Series.*

But Paul knew there was much more to his open door than improved circumstances and uncanny opportunities.

In plain language he pointed out something else that existed on the other side of the door: trouble. The entire verse reads, "A wide door for effective work has opened for me, *and there are many adversaries.*"

Unlike the passages I've mentioned with that pivotal word "yet,"this word "and" is a bold statement of fact. Yes, God can and will open miraculous doors to do His work through us, *and* you can expect trouble when you walk through those doors. "Yet" is a triumphant word, a word used in troublesome times to remind the saints to grasp hold of the surpassing joy available to us in the worst of times.

"And" just tells us to expect the worst of times . . . from time to time. *The Message* says it in a parenthetical phrase: "(There is also mushrooming opposition)." The Good News translates it this way: "even though there are many opponents." And the New Living Translation states, "although many oppose me." *Also. Even though. Although.* I think "and" is perhaps the most appropriate word. It makes Paul's statement less a warning or a lament, but rather a matter-of-fact statement of the way things are.

We soon discovered Paul was right. Trouble almost always lurks just inside the open door.

Kidnapped

There were times in our bamboo city of 150,000 citizens when people simply disappeared. Narrow rows of small houses leaned into each other between wide dirt roads. Neither the homes nor the roads had electric lights. We spent our nights indoors. When we did go out, almost no one made the short journeys between church and school and home alone. Thai soldiers patrolled the streets and insisted they remained empty after dark. Young girls had been known to vanish in the middle of the night and everyone knew why. Marauders—teenage boys, soldiers, or criminals—took them either for their own pleasure or to sell to a brothel.

Early one evening, the kind of night that had become typical in the Mam household, I went to visit a family who needed some comfort. Kanika and Sokunaroat went to a youth Bible study at the church. When I returned, I discovered only Kanika was at home. I walked the short distance to the church to walk Sokunaroat home safely and discovered she had left long before. I backtracked to our house, hoping to find her there. She wasn't. The reality quickly set in: Sokunaroat was missing.

Borin dropped by our home, and we prayed together, asking the Lord to help us find her before any real harm came to her. We then set off to the police station to report her missing. On our way, a Thai soldier stopped us and told us to go home. A general was due to pass through our section, and the streets had to be made secure. I pleaded with the officer in Thai, begging him to imagine how he would feel if his daughter was missing. He let us pass.

In the distance, we saw a group of Khmer policemen approaching. I called out so I wouldn't alarm them, and I told them I was searching for my lost daughter. I had recorded an album of nostalgic Khmer songs for the Cambodian guards in our camp, and they all recognized my name from this recording. They flanked Borin and me and escorted us directly to their police station.

Their walkie-talkies crackled as they contacted various outposts to ask if anyone had seen Sokunaroat. One man had seen another man with her. This man had taken her to the KISA (Khmer Intelligence Security Agency) headquarters. Everyone, including officials from other groups, feared the KISA. Their offices were off-limits, not only to civilians but also to the police. It looked as if, although we knew where Sokunaroat was, we couldn't get to her.

Borin and I continued to pray. We decided to contact my friend Mr. Van Roeun, the director of the School of Fine Arts, and set off to find him. Perhaps he could put me in touch with someone of influence in KISA. It was, by now, late at night. I also knew Mr. Roeun was suffering from the flu, but I was desperate.

He wrapped himself in blankets and, shivering with fever, accompanied Borin and me to the home of Mr. Ta, principal of the high school in Site II North. This man was a friend of the commander of KISA. By now it was well past midnight. Mr. Ta was in his hammock, but still awake. He told me he had wanted to meet me for some time because of my reputation as an English teacher. I could tell he wanted to converse more, but he knew this wasn't the time. Mr. Ta then took me to the home of Mr. Sak, the commander of KISA.

Amazingly, Mr. Sak didn't seem perturbed that we knocked on his door in the middle of the night. He thought my name sounded familiar and invited us in. Although I was frantic, I tried to be polite and make conversation. I asked him how old he was. We were the same age. I asked him if he had any children. He did.

"Do you have a favorite?" I asked.

"Yes, my 16-year-old son is my favorite."

"How would you feel if he went missing?"

"I wouldn't be able to sleep. I wouldn't eat. I would miss him so much."

"That's exactly how I feel right now," I said. "I love my daughter so much. Would you be so kind as to help me find her? Could you send your people into as many buildings and houses as you can to hunt for her?"

I knew that if his guards found Sokunaroat in the KISA headquarters, he would be humiliated. I gave him the opportunity to help and still save face. He felt my pain, and so he sent troops to search for her. We didn't wait long before a group of men returned to say they had not only found my daughter, they had also arrested her kidnapper. Sokunaroat and a few of the officers accompanied us back to our house where Boury and the church were gathered, waiting and praying. It was five in the morning, but we were wide-awake and wanted to hear Sokunaroat's story.

"I don't remember everything," she said. "I smelled a strange odor and must have passed out. The next thing I remember, I was on the back of a bicycle behind a man. I started to pray for Jesus to protect me and to help my family find me. Then something unusual happened: I started my period. It wasn't supposed to come for another week or two. I have never been early like that. When the man discovered that I was menstruating, he left me alone. Then I heard the guards calling my name. I knew I'd been found!"

Site II Reality TV

A few months later our friend Ali Blair introduced us to a film crew that was in Site II to film a documentary for the BBC. Soon after they arrived, they discovered that the man whose life they planned to highlight in their movie had been involved in an act of terror against the Khmer Rouge. They didn't want the film to focus on anyone who had been involved in bloodshed. They needed an innocent family, so they asked if they could film us in our home.

I served on both sides of the camera, both as a production assistant and as one of the lead "actors." The film referred to the Site II refugees as "pets in a cage." Little did we know this unflattering but accurate phrase would prompt John Major, the new prime minister of England, to raise his voice during the seemingly hopeless Cambodian peace process and plead for the release of "the pets in a cage" in Thailand.

We were delighted that the filmmakers wanted to showcase our music. Our friend Cheurn, who was blind, played the *tro* (a kind of Khmer violin), I played the flute, and Kanika sang. The film was a family affair: Boury cooked a meal on camera, Sokunaroat carried a bag of rice from the UN truck, and Shalom learned how to spell the word "aeroplane" in English. Kanika, who sang beautifully and hardly ever experienced stage fright, began to cry toward the end of her song. She was so overcome with emotion, she couldn't finish the last stanza. She and Sokoin, one of the young men who lived with us, had become romantically involved in the past few months. He observed the filming from outside our home and noticed, even from a distance, that her voice wavered unnaturally. But the producer felt Kanika's tears provided the most moving moment in the film.

I was giving private English lessons in our home the next morning when Kanika began behaving strangely. She looked at me and began to laugh in an unnatural way. She called me Dr. Luke. At first I thought she was still asleep, but it soon became evident that something was wrong. She didn't recognize any of us. Indeed, she had lost her memory altogether.

Life in our home ground to a halt. We had no idea how to help Kanika, but we knew she desperately needed help. Of course we asked the church to pray for us. But for once this seemed to backfire. Many friends came by to pray, but their words and their prayers just made things worse.

"Hmmmm. One daughter was kidnapped and another is psychotic. Maybe God is cursing your family."

"What have you done wrong? We thought you were such great Christian leaders, but surely you have sinned for this to happen in your family."

I felt like Job, with "miserable comforters" on every side. I began to feel I had to prove I was a good father, which, of course, only kept me from helping Kanika. Buddhist friends came by and offered their help. They meant well, but their solutions all involved occult practices, so we thanked them and refused. Ali Blair came to observe our daughter's behavior. She took notes and contacted friends who were nurses, doctors, and even a psychiatrist. We took Kanika to the American Rescue Committee hospital, but they weren't equipped to deal with psychological issues and sent her to another hospital. There she grew worse, and they eventually sent her back to us.

A Japanese OMF missionary named Hidiaki heard about Kanika and visited us in the camp. He suggested a simple therapy, one I was more than willing to try. He said, "Barnabas, spend some time reflecting on your relationship with Kanika and ask yourself: Have I truly supported her? Have I listened to her? Does she know I care about her?"

It would have been easy to feel defensive, but I was ready to do anything to help Kanika get better, including searching my own heart as humbly and honestly as I could. It wasn't long into this process that I realized I had not been as supportive as I thought I was.

I had been an excellent pastor to those in need. I had counseled many young people, couples, and families. But when my own children needed me, I was always too busy. Too many times, I'd said, "I am so busy, daughter. Can we talk about this later?" Because I continually put off any deep discussions, I had not realized how serious Kanika's relationship with Sokoin had become. I had been far too harsh in my handling of their romance. Sokoin had asked me for her hand in marriage, and I also put him off.

I'd told him, "When one of your brothers or sisters writes a letter to me, formally asking for her hand in marriage on your behalf, you may marry her."

This may sound reasonable, but Sokoin explained that his family still lived in Cambodia, and any letter from Thailand would only endanger them. He had one brother who lived in the United States, and he had written to him, with no response. While Kanika struggled to recover, we discovered this brother had died. Understandably, Sokoin felt I was against him. In fact, when the crew came to film life in our home, I excluded him, though he was essentially a member of the family. Of course Kanika felt this exclusion very deeply.

Kanika's healing was a slow process. But God did heal her. It began with my apology, both to her and to Sokoin. Though she didn't understand, it was necessary and helped her progress. I had a heart-to-heart talk with Sokoin and became convinced he genuinely loved my daughter. He assured me, "I will never leave her or forsake her."

He backed up those words by sticking with her as her constant companion during the toughest months of her healing. Even when Kanika acted like a child and played on the swings or with umbrellas, Sokoin joined her. Every morning, he read a chapter of 1 Corinthians from his Khmer Bible to her. By the time he finished reading the book, Kanika's memory was restored. I repeated my apology, and this time she not only understood, she also accepted it and forgave me. By the time Sokoin came to the end of 2 Corinthians, Kanika was singing again.

Before Hidiaki left Site II, he laid hands on me and prayed a prophetic prayer: "Lord, thank You for giving Barnabas such a name. Please give him the spirit of Barnabas, son of encouragement, so he will bring encouragement to many people around the world for Your glory."

I gratefully responded, "Amen!"

A Big Dream, Almost Too Big for Me

There were sixteen sections in Site II. That doesn't sound like many, but it seemed like an overwhelming number to me, especially when you consider that 150,000 people populated the entire camp—more than 9,000 in each section. I had become involved with Campus Crusade for Christ Cambodia, and the national director, Reverend Vek Huong Taing, asked if I would be the ministry leader for all of Site II.

His dream, which I fully embraced, was to develop a clear strategy to share Christ with the camp population, to make disciples of new believers, and to plant a church in each of the sections. I had already discovered the most effective strategy for evangelism was English instruction. That meant building an English school next to a church building in each of the sixteen sections.

The dream could not be accomplished through one man. I knew that. But what I didn't know was how angry people would get when I reached out to other Christians to share it.

Everything came to a head at Christmas in 1988. I still preached every Sunday, but I collapsed from exhaustion as soon as I got home. I had collaborated with Campus Crusade, the Seventh Day Adventist Church, a group of Catholics, and other secular leaders in the camp to put on a program that I hoped would bring unity to the body of Christ.

Instead, many Christians criticized me. Some of these detractors were evangelical missionaries. They accused me of having "too many heads." I responded that I had only one head—Jesus—and these other groups were simply different hats. A wise farmer wears different types of hats depending on the season and the crop he plants.

To put it bluntly: I fell apart. I could not sleep. I'm sure the coffee habit I'd developed to cope with my workload didn't help. I lost weight. I literally couldn't get out of bed. Boury ministered to me day and night. She cashed in valuables to buy medicine for me, but to no avail.

My critics then turned on her and rebuked her for her extravagant spending! They even implied that perhaps she had stolen drugs from the hospital for me. In Cambodian culture we visit the sick, bearing gifts of fresh fruit. The gifts my visitors brought were the sour fruit of criticism.

Then one day, Father Alfonso de Juan, a director of the Catholic Office for Emergency Relief and Refugees (COERR), came to see me. He was a Spanish Jesuit priest who had become a close friend. "Barnabas," he said, "don't stay mired in the past. It's making you sick with what is called psychosomatic illness. I know the root of your sickness: You are a man of vision, a big dreamer! You are disappointed in your friends and their lack of support."

I had to agree. Father Alfonso suggested I set my eyes on Jesus and on the future. He advised me to eat and sleep and rest my weary body. Like Kanika, I didn't get well immediately. It took some time. But I did heal. The next morning I heard the youth choir singing a beautiful praise song at the church just a few steps away. The song made its way into my heart, and I began to feel better.

Battle of the Bands

I became friends with the director of the KPNLF media. As digital technology made its way to the refugee camps, he struggled to make the switch from analog to digital recording. In exchange for my help in this area, he allowed me access to their recording studios. He was an advocate for us because of our friendship, but also because he listened to our music almost every day and loved it. Here was just the open door we needed to broadcast our music beyond the barbed-wire fence of Site II.

We recorded two albums, one through the evangelical church and one through the Catholic church. Daniel and I edited and mastered both albums. One day, just as we were finished and the albums were ready, my friend from KPNLF media came into the studio and looked into my eyes, but said nothing.

"What's wrong?" I asked. "Why are you sad?"

"General Kunthon just sent the order to destroy all of your recordings."[1]

Daniel and I were stunned. "Why?" I asked.

"He doesn't want your recordings released," he said, looking down at the floor. "It's because the quality of your recordings is so superior to anything the KPNLF has produced. He doesn't want the people to hear your Christian songs in Khmer traditional music at all."

I was naïve. I assumed this ridiculous request would never be carried out. Surely no one in his right mind would destroy all our hard work. Things had been looking up. We had more freedom than ever before. This sounded like an old Khmer Rouge tactic.

Daniel took action and contacted Rome. He, Father Alfonso, and another Catholic friend we called Mother Adelia worked with COERR and, through COERR, had ties to the Vatican. By communicating the situation to outsiders, Daniel protected their album. Mine, however, was destroyed.

I was heartbroken. We began to pray, and eventually we decided to use the old equipment we'd smuggled all the way from Trat to reproduce the same album. We had one stereo mixer, one analog recorder, two microphones, a few instruments, and a few digital effects processors. We built a studio in our home, using a bamboo frame, mud, and blankets. It was nothing like the KPNLF facility, but it would have to do.

Though it was doubtful we could record anything useful under these conditions, we heard General Kunthon had gotten wind of our project and wasn't happy. We stepped up production and, miraculously, ended up with a great album that matched the quality of the one that had been destroyed. This time, I knew better than to assume it was safe. So I quickly sent it to the FEBC Radio in Manila.

The next week, the *Tinh Lan* church asked to use our equipment. They were able to record only a few Vietnamese carols before bandits stole everything we had loaned them and badly beat our Vietnamese brothers. The next morning we recovered the microphones near the Vietnamese section, but we never found the recorder.

No, everything isn't always resolved. But I have found that God does not waste sorrow. He uses trouble for His glory.

Father Alfonso felt so badly for us and our ill-fated musical pursuits, he asked how he could help. I wasn't sure he could do anything, but he immediately began trying to find a replacement for our Sony TC-D5M recorder. By this time analog equipment was all but obsolete. Father Alfonso ordered a Sony recorder just like ours from Bangkok, but they were sold out. He ordered one from Singapore, but same story. Finally he got one for us from Hong Kong. He also graciously granted me a significant amount of COERR cultural funds so I could buy the equipment and instruments I needed to better operate my recording studio. We continued to make music until the day we left Site II.

The Other Side of "And"

When God opens a door and trouble ensues, there is always an epilogue. That's how the story goes. No, everything isn't always resolved and wrapped in a neat package. You could not have read this far and still believe that. But I have found that God does not waste sorrow. He uses trouble for His glory. There is another side to "and."

When the guards returned Sokunaroat safely to us, something incredible happened at Site II. The camp administrators got wind of the incident right away. They were stunned by the number of people who helped look for her or who gathered to pray. Their response was to immediately set new policies against sex trafficking and abuse. The UN and the Red Cross got involved too and, along with the administration, raised the standard campwide on behalf of Cambodian girls. Although I would never in a million years choose to endure that ordeal, God used it for the sake of many other Cambodian women.

Both Kanika and I suffered emotionally. My pain was so deep, it affected me physically. I discovered an open door for effective work within my weakness. I'm not sure our family would have had the inroads into the lives of others who suffer if we hadn't ourselves suffered. In his second letter to the Corinthians, Paul praises the God "who comforts us in all our troubles, so that we can comfort those in any trouble with the comfort we ourselves have received from God" (2 Corinthians 1:4 NIV). Not only did God forge in us a deeper compassion for the hurting, He also opened an even wider door.

In 1990 Father Alfonso graciously dipped into the COERR funds for Hope English School. We built a school in the premises of each of our evangelical churches all over Site II. The schools were equipped with an audio lab, a library, and qualified English teachers. Many young people attended these schools, and as a result many could read, write, and speak English by the time they left the camp. Those who were interested in the Christian faith were discipled by Campus Crusade staffers who were sent to work with us. COERR engaged an English teacher to be their liaison officer with Hope English School.

In 1991 Reverend Arun Sok Nhep and Father François Ponchaud, translators of Today's Khmer Version (now known as the Khmer Standard Version) for the Bible Society, visited me in Site II. They asked me to proofread their new translation. I gladly agreed. The three of us created Khmer abbreviations for the names of each book of the Bible.

Remember my prayer in 1972? When I purchased my first Bible, I asked the Lord to make me a translator and teacher of His Word. My work on this translation was the beginning of God's answer to that plea. When we returned to Phnom Penh, I became the vice chairman of the Bible Society in Cambodia and held that post for six years. Next, I served as chairman for ten years.

In 1992 a woman named Phally, one of my English students and the founder of the Khmer People Depression Relief Center at Site II, approached me about working as an adviser to the center's programs. By this time, everyone understood that depression was the inevitable result of all our wanderings.

My only training in the art of healing mingled herbal therapy with the occult practices I had learned as a child from my father. I wondered what I had to offer, but I sensed this was something I had to do. COERR engaged a professional social worker named Claudia Fisher to be their liaison officer with the center. She helped me incorporate biblical truth with traditional herbal remedies without venturing into the occult. She was an evangelical believer in Christ, and I learned a lot about counseling from her.

Later a group from the School of Mental Health at Harvard University, led by Dr. Richard Mollica, visited Site II. These mental health workers brought a depth of knowledge and experience to our efforts. In addition, Dr. Mollica invited Phally, Claudia Fisher, two other Cambodian mental health workers, and me to attend a World

Congress on Migrants and Mental Health in Rome. By this time, in 1992, travel outside of the camp was a bit easier, and we were given permission. Our newly acquired skills not only broadened the work at the center, but they would also be useful when peace came and we went home to Cambodia.

Phally's husband was a remarkable gardener and used his skill to coax lovely plants, herbs, and flowers out of the dusty soil at the center. Boury got some rose plants from him to cultivate in our front yard. They looked so beautiful and smelled so sweet. The Depression Relief Center became a calm oasis of beauty and color for the hurting. Our work garnered the attention of the many NGOs, the hospital workers, and the authorities in the camp. Soon we were almost overrun with referrals. Typically these were patients who continually attempted suicide and seemed unreachable, even to the experts. I kept a list of the names of these patients so my family and I could pray for them.

Mr. Bunsat had been a captain in the KPNLF army. He often left his family behind in Site II to fight in various sorties on the other side of the border in Cambodian territory. The enemy he fought against depended on where the fighting took place: either the Vietnamese or forces of the People's Republic of Kampuchea. Mr. Bunsat became quite wealthy because he nearly always brought home loot from the battlefield.

One rainy day as his squadron was traveling back to the camp, his truck slipped off the road and collided with another vehicle. Mr. Bunsat was trapped beneath his truck. He cried out to his fellow soldiers. Several times a few soldiers approached him, and each time Mr. Bunsat thought his rescue was imminent. But rather than help him, these men rifled through his pockets for valuables. Finally, two men freed him from the truck. That's when Mr. Bunsat discovered he was paralyzed from the waist down. The two men carried him back to his family at Site II.

Mr. Bunsat was bitter. He blamed his wife for urging him to plunder the pockets of fallen soldiers. He blamed the health workers, even though he refused their help. He blamed the army. He curled up in his bed and plotted a way to end a life that he felt certain would only sink deeper and deeper into a misery he couldn't endure. He almost succeeded. He tried poison, a gun held directly against his temple, and a razor across his throat—yet he failed. He now blamed a weakened right hand and a crafty son who removed every dangerous object from their home.

My friend Mark Erickson, a pharmacist in a camp hospital run by Youth With a Mission (YWAM), heard of Bunsat's condition. Knowing that Bunsat had refused all help, Mark prayed a few days before attempting to see him. Mark and I went together to visit him at his home. When his wife opened their door, I called out, "Mr. Bunsat, I have brought an American named Mark to visit you. Would you welcome the two of us—an American and a Cambodian pastor—to visit you in your home?"

His wife and son were astonished when Mr. Bunsat uttered a quiet "Yes." I knew then that God had saved his life. I spent the next hour telling him the story of a man who was left behind on a cross, betrayed by His friends, forsaken by all His people. For the first time, Bunsat saw pain that was greater than his own.

He said, "I want to become a Christian, but how? I can't get up and walk to church."

"Don't worry," I said. "You can become a Christian right now, right here."

Mr. Bunsat and I became brothers in Christ. Gone was his desire to end his life. Gone, too, the bitterness that had poisoned his relationships. I sent a Bible and books for him to read, plus tapes and a tape recorder so he could listen to music. He began to grow in his faith. On the other side of my "and" was a man who needed a wounded healer like me to understand his pain and share with him the good news.

The same year I met Mr. Bunsat, I entered another open door. This time, the effective work it afforded began inside of me. Reverend Chhon Phan Kong invited me to attend the CCS (Cambodian Christian Services) annual conference in Bangkok. Things were loosening up in Site II, and I was able to get a travel document to go to Bangkok for three months. Little did I know these meetings would begin a much-needed rehabilitation in my own spirit.

While there I met many Cambodian Christian leaders from all over the world and a senior C&MA missionary named Cliff Westergren, who had visited me in Site II in 1986 and commissioned me to minister to the Vietnamese church in *Trai Moi*. Cliff was gifted in counseling Christians to reconcile their differences.

The criticisms I had endured had not ceased in the intervening years, and I was so hurt and wearied by them. Westergren hosted a series of reconciliation meetings between me and other Christian leaders, some who had been the most critical. Like a father urging his children to get along, Cliff walked us through the process of asking for and giving forgiveness. He even counseled some of them to honor me and make restitution to me as a part of the process of repentance.

Later that year, an old friend named Ung Sophal from California visited me in Site II. He came with General Dien Del, who had met me in November 1985, one day after we arrived at Site II camp. Sophal spent two days ministering to me and my young leaders. He ran a ministry in Cambodia called Global Network. Knowing we would soon return to Cambodia, he updated me on the situation of the church and the government at home. He kindly offered his ministry house in Phnom Penh for my family to stay for a few months before we found a place of our own. His offer gave me hope and eased my fears about repatriation.

Soon we, the church, would begin our journey home. The door would open, and we would return to grow the body of Christ in Cambodia as never before. By now, we knew that door would have its share of "ands" behind it, but we also knew God was in the "ands" just as surely as He was in the open door.

Note

1. General Hing Kunthon died in Thailand before the KPNLF and the displaced people in Site II were welcomed back home to Cambodia.

Chapter Seventeen

CAMP COMMUNITY

The Church Learns to Love Holistically

I think music in itself is healing. It's an explosive
expression of humanity. It's something we are all
touched by. No matter what culture we're from,
everyone loves music.

—Billy Joel

The time has come for a revival of public worship as the
finest of the fine arts . . . While there is a call for
strong preaching there is even a greater
need for uplifting worship.

—Andrew W. Blackwood

Sing to him a new song;
play skillfully, and shout for joy.

—Psalm 33:3 NIV

PARISIAN Elyse Schein and New Yorker Paula Bernstein blush about the same things. The movements their hands make when they fidget are mirror images. They have the same drug allergies. The list of their uncanny commonalities goes on and on. But the strangest similarities of all are these: their birth date, their birthplace, and their birth mother. Elyse and Paula are identical twins who were separated by an adoption agency at birth. Because they share the same DNA, Elyse and Paula also share a host of specific characteristics, even though they never got a chance to learn them from each other. They didn't meet until after their thirty-fifth birthday.[1]

You could say the Cambodian church had been separated for a long time from her sister, the rest of the church worldwide. We were torn from each other during the years of the Killing Fields and later, as the church in Phnom Penh experienced a quiet, painful rebirth underground. We began to reconnect during our years of exile, slowly and haltingly. Like Elyse Schein and Paula Bernstein, when we finally met to compare the notes of our disparate lives, we were surprised to find we'd learned many of the same lessons while we were apart. We were sisters, after all.

Identical Church Growth

During the late 1970s and '80s, the Lausanne Conference, influenced heavily by leaders like Billy Graham and theologian John Stott, led the international evangelical church to minister across racial barriers, to meet not only spiritual needs but also physical and emotional ones. The church, as it became more global, also became more holistic. No one redefined biblical mission, but many were learning to expand it.

If the church was going to be a community of salt and light within the larger community, we had to love aggressively and boldly.

Although we couldn't know it at first, the church in Site II was growing parallel to the church in the free world.

Our neighbors were diametrically different from us, if not our traditional enemies, as many were. We were charged by Jesus to love our neighbors: the lepers, the Vietnamese, the Muslims, and the Buddhists; the depressed and the hungry; and, to use a term that fit all of us, the war-torn. Our neighbors needed the gospel, to be sure. But they also needed just about everything else.

We couldn't escape Site II, and we couldn't escape the needy world at our doorstep. We were packed into such close quarters, our lives intersected every day. If the church was going to be a community of salt and light within the larger community, we had to love aggressively and boldly. The radical love of our Savior, expressed in as many ways possible, was the only way to tear down the walls between us.

Giving Everything and Wasting Nothing

Men in Site II, single or married, could not receive food rations. If they had no family, they had no real means of getting any unless they joined the KPNLF army. The primary emotion of refugee life for young women was fear; for the young men it was helplessness and shame. Although I'm sure it was a blow to their pride, many of these men relied on the mercy of the church.

Sanith was one such man whose basic needs were provided by a family in our church in section 14. Sanith was so impressed by the generosity of the body of Christ that he also wanted to learn to give. He asked me if there was any way he could be obedient to the Lord and give sacrificially, even without resources. He felt his intentions were thwarted because he had nothing to offer.

I reassured him he had plenty to give. He could spend his time and his talents for others. There certainly was plenty to do. I then asked him to carry the water, split the firewood, and cook food for our Saturday morning school. As we began to plant churches in each of the sixteen sections of Site II, we realized the young pastors needed to know how to study the Scriptures and how to preach. So we had established the Saturday school.

Sanith was a hard worker. He quickly learned how to choose the menu, regulate the heat of the fire, and serve the food at the proper time. He was also faithful, never missing a Saturday. Eventually I began to teach him, using his weekly chores as an analogy for the work of the pastor. Yes, it was important for a preacher to craft a sermon from the right ingredients, but we needed the fire of the Holy Spirit if we were going to serve truth with power.

Sharing and giving became "business as usual" for Sanith. It also became a defining characteristic of the church. Years later, after I had helped found Living Hope in Christ Church in Phnom Penh and it was time for me to hand off the pastorate, Sanith was my natural choice for the job. I knew him to be faithful in small things like hauling water and cooking a meal over a fire. He also proved to be faithful in the larger work of the ministry.

Love on the Outside

It is one thing to share among believers. But just as the Israelites stored up manna in the wilderness and discovered it became rancid when they hoarded it, the body of Christ won't grow if we confine giving to safe, easy sacrifice among ourselves. We might even sour. We're called to love outside our own four walls, and that's when it can get a little messy.

Jean Clavaud was a French missionary working with

the Christian and Missionary Alliance in Cambodia before 1975. Clavaud and his family were permitted to stay
in the country after most groups were driven out in 1965
simply because they were not Americans. He was known
for his compassion. He was arrested by the Khmer Rouge
in Takeo Province and detained for a few months in the
early 1970s.

But that isn't what makes Jean Chavaud stand out from
his fellow missionaries of that era. Many of his colleagues
misunderstood him because he devoted so much of his
time to the Buddhist monks in many of the *wats* in Phnom
Penh. He developed relationships with monks and taught
them French and English. He was also a powerful example to me. Not only did Jean Clavaud love his neighbors, the Buddhist monks, he was also willing to incur the
disapproval of other Christians because of that love.

Venerable Muni Chenda, a brilliant young monk who
was well-known in Site II, invited me and my musician
friend, Svay Sor, to establish a school of music in *Wat
Prasat Serei.* We were delighted. We recruited teachers
and students and, as a result, cemented our friendships
with many of the monks. Later when I began preaching
in the Vietnamese section of the camp, I would often drop
by their *wat* after our service.

One day the *mekun,* or chief abbot, of *Wat Khmer
Krom* in *Trai Moi* invited me to have lunch with him in the
wat. After lunch, he revealed that he would be leaving for

the United States soon and he had a favor to ask. Would I teach English to the community of monks in his *wat*? He asked if we might tape our sessions and my translations of some of the English books in their library. He added, "We will always say on these tapes that this session was kindly provided by our good friend Pastor Barnabas in Site II." That was quite an honor.

Before lunch the *mekun* had shown me an even greater honor. Before the meal, he introduced me to the other monks and said, "Barnabas is not just a pastor of one church. He oversees many churches just as I oversee many Buddhist *wats* in South Vietnam. So Barnabas is a *mekun* in a Christian context; he is not lesser than I."

I found it touching that my new friend understood so well who I was. But he wasn't finished: "You honor me. Honor him as well. You respect me. Respect him too. I have invited him to eat a meal with us. Christian pastors never eat food that has been already offered to the spirits. We Buddhists do, but they don't, so this meal has not been offered to the spirits. Pastor Barnabas, you may enjoy it freely."

The friendship between the church and the *wat* didn't stop here. It began to seep into all aspects of our shared culture. The church in Site II was not recognized by the Thai government. That meant we were not given a place to conduct services or bury our dead. The only place we could hold funeral services was in the crematorium at

Wat Prasat Serei. It turned out to be a good place to lead our services in the Cambodian manner.

I learned that the Buddhists believed Western musical instruments were not acceptable for funeral services. So I wrote a Khmer-style poem for funerals that could be chanted as the Buddhists chant. The poem answered the questions: What is life about? Why do we need God? What is the afterlife like? I also wrote the Lord's Prayer as a song to be chanted. In effect, I was remembering the lost music of my youth. I was combining the "new song" God had taught my heart with the "old songs" we all knew from the days before the Killing Fields.

All this came into focus when an older woman died in the camp. She was an evangelical believer whose husband was Catholic, as were half of her children. The family asked for a Catholic priest to join me in conducting her service. It was a big funeral, with three hundred mourners attending. The entire local community was there. When the people heard us chant Cambodian poems with biblical meaning, they realized we were not trying to destroy their traditions and culture.

Who could blame them for suspecting us? For years Christianity was associated with Western imperialism. The Americans bombed our countryside and backed Lon Nol in his overthrow of our government. This funeral gave us an opportunity to prove that our intentions were to give, not to take.

There were still times when the collision of our cultures created misunderstandings. Weddings in Cambodia are just as tradition-filled as funerals. Many couples consider this the most important day of their lives, and they will save for a long time in order to celebrate dressed as a prince and a princess for one day. Two Christians asked me to perform their wedding ceremony.

The groom's mother, although she was Buddhist, gave her permission for them to marry. I knew that could be a problem, so I had checked to be sure she had really given her consent. But in the middle of her son's vows to his new wife, just as he uttered them "in the name of Jesus," this woman produced a knife and shouted, "If you insist on marrying this girl in the Christian way, I am no longer your mother!" Then she added, with a flourish of her kitchen knife, "If you continue, I will kill myself!"

That halted the proceedings. We were frozen in a moment of panic. I suddenly realized that the memory—one most of us shared—of the rushed weddings performed by the Khmer Rouge had a greater influence on our feelings about such ceremonies than any of us realized. It also began to dawn on me that the best aspects of our cultures come from God. Any feature of culture that honors truth is ultimately of God.

Before the entire situation got out of control, I asked both the bride and groom to kneel, facing the groom's mother. I whispered some instruction to the man, and he looked up at me with an understanding smile. In the Cambodian fashion, he bowed three times before his mother. He then said to her, "Thank you. Thank you, Mom, for raising me from infancy to adulthood. I know you love me so much. Your sacrificial love is the reason I survived and live today. Thank you for encouraging me to marry my wife. Both of us want to thank you."

By celebrating together
the many milestones in our lives,
—funerals, weddings, and births—
the church developed
a platform for the gospel.

His bride nodded with a tentative smile toward the woman she had thought, until moments before, embraced her as a daughter-in-law. The knife clattered to the ground as the mother dropped it and embraced both young people. The three of them hugged and wept until the groom pulled away and asked, "Mom, will you accept your new daughter-in-law? As Christians, we are taught by our Lord Jesus to love you, to respect you, and to honor you. If we do that, the Lord will bless us."

The answer was as obvious as the tears of joy on the

mother's face. She later confided to me that she had been warned by friends in the camp that Christians no longer love their parents after they marry. She was relieved to discover this was not the case.

Today in Cambodia, many Christian wedding ceremonies integrate this traditional practice of bowing in respect to the parents, along with another old Cambodian custom, foot washing. Traditionally, the bride washes the groom's feet. But in an attempt to reflect a more biblical picture, the groom also washes the bride's feet in Christian ceremonies. Christian couples dress as Cambodians have at weddings for centuries, as a prince and a princess instead of in a white dress and tuxedo, a practice unknown to us until Western missionaries introduced it. And why not? We're royalty: "But you are a chosen people, a royal priesthood, a holy nation, a people belonging to God, that you may declare the praises of him who called you out of darkness into his wonderful light" (1 Peter 2:9 NIV). Being called out of darkness doesn't necessarily mean we are called away from our culture, it means we can view it in a brand-new, wonderful light.

The Sound of a Community Set Free

What does it mean to be a community? At the core, it means to know and be known, to serve and be served, to love and be loved, and to celebrate and be celebrated. This is what community began to look like in Site II. By celebrating the many milestones in our lives together, the church developed perhaps the best platform for the gospel. Teaching English merely shared information. Funerals, weddings, the birth of a baby; these events allowed us to share *life*.

One common denominator of our celebrations was music. I composed and performed music that struck the same sentimental chord inside all of us. When a new baby arrived in a home, we celebrated using a Khmer lullaby with biblical lyrics. I recorded Khmer folk songs for the soldiers who wanted to hear the sound of home. Not only did God use music to speak truth to those in Site II who did not know Him, music also became a harbinger of hope. Music reminded us of home and the hope that we would one day return there. For Christians, worshiping God in song was a taste of our heavenly home. For all of us, music became a taste of our Cambodian home. One day we would go back. Until that day, although God had not yet returned us to our country, He returned our country's music to us.

Sometimes our music made its way to places of its own accord. Sometimes God used it to minister in ways we could never have predicted. There were those in Site II whose plight, like the lepers or the poor or the hungry, was far worse than ours. They needed to hear a hopeful song more than anyone. But we didn't always know who those people were.

Our family was blessed in that the guides who led us from Phnom Penh to Thailand were, for the most part, trustworthy. But not everyone who ended up in Site II was as fortunate as we were. There were vast networks of guides who were nothing more than petty blackmailers. These men would offer to lead a family to one of the refugee camps for a very small fee. The family, usually quite desperate, would fall prey to the allure of the low price and entrust everything to these guides.

Once they made it to the camp, the men would hold their charges hostage. They would then force them to contact family or friends who lived in the "third countries" by phone for ransom money. (Cambodians consider our own country the first country, Thailand the second, and America or Australia the third.) This hardly ever worked out the way the "guides" planned it, and many of the unwitting families would then be marched back across the border to be executed.

For a long time we were unaware of this practice, but after a while we began to hear reports of it. Whenever a neighborhood got wind that yet another group of duped men and women were being held on their street, the kidnappers' message got out loud and clear: if you help our enemies, we will kill you. Many of the corrupt guides were KPNLF soldiers for whom extortion was a lucrative side job. And many of their victims were their traditional enemies, the Vietnamese.

During the weeks of my health breakdown, unknown to us, a group of five hostages were languishing in a makeshift prison cell in a house down the street from ours. These prisoners had no hope of rescue—and we had no idea they were there. They were Vietnamese Catholic believers literally walled into an inside room with no way out. Yet through the walls of their small windowless cell, they heard us singing hymns on Sunday mornings. They heard our youth choir practicing on Saturdays. They heard the children singing every day at the Hope Christian School.

Though I was too sick to get out of bed, the young pastors I mentored met every morning at my bedside to pray. One such morning, as we pounded on the gates of hell in our prayers, the prisoners decided to pull down the walls of their prison. We were still praying when they rushed up to my bedroom window, grasped its bars, and cried out: "Help us! We are Christians too!"

Their captors were close behind. We watched in dismay as a few KPNLF soldiers pried the men's hands off my window and carried them away. As they dragged their prey by their arms, they shouted the familiar words back at us: "If you help our enemies, we will kill you."

I was so proud of the young men who were with me that morning. There was no question in their minds; we would help. They wasted no time and slipped out of my house to call on some of the UN officers they knew. Soon

Bob Mat, a Catholic brother in Christ who served with UN security, and my friend Claudia Fisher arrived at the house, and we prayed together about what to do. It seemed hopeless, and no one had any good ideas.

As we prayed, the thought came to me that we might be able to reach the captors' families and plead with them to return their prisoners. We used Bob's walkie-talkie to get in touch with them and begged them to help us. I'm not sure I expected it to work, but it did. Every one of the men returned. They were badly beaten, each missing a few teeth, but they were safe. The blackmailers were eventually apprehended and dealt with by the camp's now-improved court system. Because the victims were all Catholics, their story was relayed to their aid agency, COERR. The result was a deeper friendship between evangelical and Catholic believers.

This incident occurred during a time when I was, physically and emotionally, at my worst. Maybe I needed a shock to my system, but after the rescue of our Vietnamese brothers, I began to heal. I found I could again make music. And what music we began to make! Boury supported our work by cooking for the musicians. Kanika was her old self again and sang with us. Sokunaroat also lent her beautiful voice. Shalom participated in our prayer times.

God was using us in mighty ways. We were at once humbled and amazed. Little by little, note by note, the dream of a church in every one of the sixteen sections in Site II began to come true. And as each church emerged, we worshiped together in song. We didn't sing because we could—as many do in the free world—we sang because we couldn't help it.

Note

1. Elyse Schein and Paula Bernstein, *Identical Strangers: A Memoir of Twins Separated and Reunited* (New York: Random House, 2008).

Chapter Eighteen

THE MARCH
TOWARD PEACE

And the Long March Home

Lord, bid war's trumpet cease;
Fold the whole earth in peace.

—Oliver Wendell Holmes

Let us forgive each other—
only then will we live in peace.

—Leo Tolstoy

It is more difficult to organize a peace than to win
a war; but the fruits of victory will be lost
if the peace is not organized.

—Aristotle

So then let us pursue what makes for peace
and for mutual upbuilding.

—Romans 14:19

POLITICAL powers erect walls. And these walls always represent the same thing: a woefully inadequate alternative to peace. The Iron Curtain and its tropical cousin, the Bamboo Curtain, were symbolic walls between countries that could not find their way to lasting peace. The literal walls along the border between Thailand and Cambodia that kept us from entering our own homeland seemed to us like they might stay in place for decades.

Then something happened in another country in another hemisphere that gave us hope. We had been behind our barbed-wire walls for less than a decade. East Germans had lived behind theirs for almost four decades.

When the Berlin Wall went up in 1961, it looked a lot like the wall around Site II. But soon the barbed wire was replaced by miles and miles of impenetrable reinforced concrete. German engineering at its best produced a wall so strong that a car couldn't drive through it. The open field of raked gravel called the Death Strip, which ensured the guards that no one could approach without leaving their footprints behind as evidence, the many watchtowers, the "bed of nails" under each of its balconies; all these features guaranteed the Berlin Wall would keep the inhabitants of East Germany "safe" for years and years to come.

Surely these citizens of another country, enclosed by another wall, were our brothers in captivity. Surely their situation was as hopeless, if not more so, as ours.

Like us, East Germans were not without advocates. President Ronald Reagan, in a speech at the Brandenburg Gate in 1987, made a public entreaty: "We welcome change and openness; for we believe that freedom and security go together, that the advance of human liberty can only strengthen the cause of world peace . . . Mr. Gorbachev, open this gate. Mr. Gorbachev, tear down this wall!"

> God began to tear down the walls I had erected that kept peace out of my own life. Only then could I genuinely preach and pray about peace.

It would be two more years before the wall actually came down. But it did, and we were ecstatic. If it could happen in Germany, it could happen here.

Next Year in Phnom Penh

We took our cues from Germany. We knew the church there had prayed for the destruction of the wall, so we began to pray for the destruction of the walls that kept us out of Cambodia. Even before the UN began gathering the different political factions to discuss peace in Paris, we gathered more than five hundred adults, along with two hundred children, to a service where we prayed for peace. Some stayed all night to pray.

I have no doubt that God answers prayers. But sometimes His answers are far deeper and more complex than we can imagine. Sometimes His answers are uncomfortably personal. My prayers for peace proved to be no exception.

You can't pray very effectively for something for others if you aren't willing to experience it yourself. To be honest, I wasn't fully at peace. It's no wonder many of us weren't. The grave injustices that had been committed against us by the Khmer Rouge had dug into the soil of our hearts, and the poisonous plants of bitterness and unforgiveness began to grow. We were praying for peace, but we weren't peaceful.

In that wonderfully circuitous miracle of prayer, God began to tear down the walls I had erected that kept peace out of my own life. Only then could I genuinely and powerfully preach and pray about peace. Only then could I respond with grace to my detractors within the body of Christ. And only then could I watch with unadulterated joy as former Khmer Rouge *cadres* began to meet Christ and join our churches in Site II and later in Phnom Penh.

James says, "Confess your sins to each other and pray for each other so that you may be healed. The earnest prayer of a righteous person has great power and produces wonderful results" (James 5:16 NLT). The "righteous person" God used to pray with me was Mark Erickson.

Mark was a missionary with Youth With a Mission (YWAM), a group our network of churches collaborated with quite often. Once we became friends, Mark started coming to our home every afternoon at 4:30 for prayer. If I could not meet him, Boury and Shalom always did. More and more of the leaders in the church began to join us. These leaders were Chea Sothea, Uon Seila, Touch Borin, Ray Sano, That Bunthoeun, Chhoy Chhin, Houl Norin, Thach Somantha, Ke Tha, Sath Sokha, Say Setha, and Kruoch Sarath. I credit these times of prayer and Mark's counsel with the final uprooting of my own anger and bitterness against the Khmer Rouge. Not only did God heal me, He also led me to forgive as only a man set free can do.

Another influence on my life during these days was the example of Wang Ming Dao, a Chinese brother in Christ who spent twenty-two years in prison for his refusal to join the Three-Self Patriotic Movement of the state-controlled churches. While in prison, Dao developed a deep longing for the return of Jesus, saying to himself, "Maranatha! The Lord is coming soon!" He wrote that this grew out of the hopeful phrase the Israelites used while in captivity: "Next year in Jerusalem." I modified this phrase and made it the theme of our final year in Site II. I began telling our family and the church, "Next year in Phnom Penh." I said it so often, they began to believe me.

Preparing for Peace

Peace was on its way. Maybe it wasn't rolling in like a thunderous victory parade, but everyone in the camp knew something was stirring. The UN had begun making their overtures from Paris to Cambodia. Inside Site II, the UN convened meetings of various refugee groups to begin human rights training. I was often asked to be a part of these meetings. I learned from the experts about the negative experiences of refugees that weigh against that one stunning positive: going home.

Many refugees receive better food, health care, and education in the camps than those who stayed home. This can easily lead to resentment between groups. Because the refugees may return with a command of English and other benefits, they often become leaders, they get the best jobs, and they are naturally propelled beyond those who stayed. We didn't know if this would happen with us, but we needed to be prepared for it.

There was a lot we didn't know. Our children, many of them born in Site II, did not know anything about the country we so fondly remembered. The very act of describing "home" to them produced more questions. Shalom couldn't remember Cambodia or what it was like to live there. For Shalom, food arrived in a truck with the letters "UN" stenciled on its flank. She had never seen an ox or a cart. She had never seen a rice paddy! For a while throughout the camp, lessons in history and geography took precedence over everything else. When I told Shalom there were sugar palm trees in Cambodia, she could not picture what a palm tree looked like. I tried to describe them, but I finally had to tell her, "One day, I'll show you one."

Another concern was the land mines. We hoped the international community would help us remove them, but we knew the danger was there, just under the surface of our fields and our forests. What I feared most was not the physical possibility that we might, at any moment, step on one of those deadly concealed weapons. I feared the hornet's nest of hatred that I knew lurked in the hearts of so many. Could we really achieve peace in a land still so fraught with danger?

Later, we would ask God to afford us this same kind of recognition and freedom once we were home in Cambodia.

I wasn't sure how our country would fare, but I felt it was now my responsibility, as a pastor to many pastors throughout Site II, to make sure the church marched back into Cambodia as bearers of peace. If we could do that, I knew we could have an impact on the rest of our nation for peace.

We decided to prepare the church to focus on two areas: indigenous worship and adult education. We would give the music of Cambodia back to our people through our worship. And we would ensure, through the education of our leaders, our men and women, and our children, that the Cambodian people would never again be as vulnerable to the kind of deceit the Khmer Rouge used against us.

The Khmer Evangelical Church in Site II became a voice for human rights. As a result, the UN called on me often to interpret for them. At these meetings many of our questions about repatriation were bandied about. How would we be classified? And would these classifications (labeling us as members of the warring factions) only endanger us further? How would we get home? Where would we go once we got there? Back to our original villages or to the decaying cities the Khmer Rouge had destroyed? Would we regain the land we'd owned before 1975? Would the Buddhists be free to march and chant? What about Christians? Would we be free to meet for worship? The more the meetings, the more questions arose.

Military skirmishes just outside our walls continued, and the wounded or dead were brought to Site II hospitals right under our noses. This understandably made people skeptical about peace. Even so, on December 10,

1989, Human Rights Day, UNBRO held a celebration in anticipation of peace. Less than a year later, in August 1990, the UN and the four parties in Cambodia reached an agreement.

But for now, we would celebrate anyway. I was asked to speak. Ten thousand people gathered. We hadn't expected anywhere near that many when we made copies of the speaking notes for my message, "Put Your Sword Back into Its Place" from Matthew 26:52, to distribute later. That day I found out each speaker was allotted only fifteen minutes. I asked the UNBRO authorities if I might tack on enough time for our choir to sing a few numbers. I had planned on leading them in folk songs as well as gospel songs. They gave me full permission, not only for my choir to sing but also to "preach whatever is written in your text, you have plenty of time."

Later, we would ask God to afford us this same kind of recognition and freedom once we were home in Cambodia. After I finished my speech, a young man named Sano said, "Pastor Barnabas, I believe that the Cambodian Christians will one day be recognized and be given freedom by the Cambodian government as we are now in Site II." To that I said a hearty "Amen!"

One of the musicians in the camp, who had been well-known before his exile and now produced music for the KPNLF Radio, found me after the choir sang. He said he had been moved by the lyrics of one of our songs: "I have given you a new commandment—love one another as I have loved you."

"I have never thought of music in this way," he said, in tears.

"What do you mean?"

"Your music mobilizes people to become a community of love," he said. "I have never seen music used that way. You have inspired me to do the same."

Although this man was successful by most standards, he admitted his sense of failure. He had trained many other musicians who were also successful, but he envied the unity that was evident among the older and younger pastors who held hands and sang together, clearly meaning every word.

Preparing to Pastor

After my conversation with the musician on Human Rights Day, I began to think a lot about what it meant to, as he said, mobilize a community of love. I remembered the apostle Paul's example. Before he left a city where he had planted a church, he would typically gather the church leaders and entrust them with the word of grace. I decided it was time to do the same in Site II. We would be leaving soon.

I called together all of the leaders under the age of 40 and gave them the practical instructions I felt they would need as they ministered in Cambodia:

- Get training in a vocation while you are still here and the training is available. That way, you can get a job and support yourself, your family, and your ministry in Cambodia.
- Work on your English. Unless you pastor a church in a rural area, you will need it.
- You will probably return empty-handed. Work hard and know that you are not alone. Though you may not have a home or an income when you first arrive, know that your heavenly Father cares for you. Remember that you were empty-handed when you left home.
- If you come to a village where a church already exists, don't plant another one in competition. Serve joyfully alongside the pastor there, just as David served Saul until it was the proper time for him to lead.

During this time, we also established seven core values and taught them to our church leaders and pastors. In formulating these values, we always had in mind the new convert, as well as the leader who would implement them:

1. *Meaningful Fellowship.* The church doesn't need high-sounding theology as much as we need each other. Build a loving environment where the rejected are loved and nurtured.

2. *Intimate Worship.* A new believer must know God personally and deeply as a friend, but also maintain a sense of His majesty.

3. *Powerful Prayer.* I later wondered why prayer meetings are so poorly attended in the West. Without intercessory prayer, there can be no church growth.

4. *Cheerful Giving.* Even in places of poverty, giving is essential. This is why holistic ministry is so important. Working in partnership with missionaries, our leaders can provide ways for even the most impoverished to earn money in order to give.

5. *Hearty Participation.* We are each part of the royal priesthood, therefore everyone must be encouraged to take part in the ministry of the church.

6. *Joyful Service.* Nothing exhibits the attitude of Philippians 2:3, "in humility count others more significant than yourselves," more than serving others.

7. *Effective Evangelism.* We are called to take the good news of Jesus, the Savior of the entire world, to others. In our country, the misconception that Christianity is a Western religion can be changed only by effective evangelism.

On October 23, 1991, the Paris Conference assembled to sign a comprehensive settlement giving the UN full authority to supervise a cease-fire. The agreement called for a disarmament and demobilization of the factional armies.

Preparations were begun, under UN supervision, for free and fair elections. The parties also agreed to repatriate all displaced Khmer along the border with Thailand. It was official: we were going home.

Chapter Nineteen

HOMEWARD
BOUND

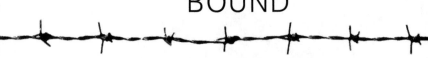

Fighting the Battle
with Fear along the Way

O Lord, you have always been our home.

—Psalm 90:1 GNT

Home is the place where,
when you have to go there,
They have to take you in.

—Robert Frost, in *The Death of the Hired Man*

WHEN I was a small boy, I often sat with my mother and counted the stars. It's hard for someone who grew up in or near a city to imagine how black the Cambodian sky appeared over our village—especially when the moon was reluctant to shine. If anything could penetrate the cloak of protection I felt in my parents' arms, the vast night sky could do it. It was just all too, well, *beyond*. The universe was unknowable and large. But my mother and I could make light of that fact by numbering the innumerable. We assigned human measurement to an immeasurable expanse. Sharing this impossible task with my mother made me feel safe and secure. In the shelter of her embrace, I could laugh at the night and tally the stars.

But even my mother could not protect me from everything. One balmy evening, as we stargazed together, a line of tiny red lights appeared near the horizon. The foreign lights grew larger. My mother explained that those lights were strung on the wings of something I'd never seen before, an airplane. She then described planes to me in a way that made sense out of the flickering lights above. I was fascinated. The lights came closer and soon outsized the stars. At the same time a rushing noise interrupted the familiar thrum of the outdoors. Flashing red lights and a deafening roar, now impossibly low, swooped over our home. And then disappeared.

We heard the plane crash in the paddy field nearby. Heard it, felt it, and almost immediately began to smell its smoke. By now the entire village was outside and, with an instinct born of both helpfulness and horror, headed toward the crash. I followed.

What I saw is still with me. The paddy field smoldered. The dismembered body of the pilot, intact enough to recognize each part, littered the ground. The fuselage of the airplane was blown into a wider circumference than seemed possible. It was my first introduction to fear, and what an introduction it was. Every time I board a plane—which is often these days—I fight the phobia I know is rooted in that night.

"How Many More?"

Shalom was just twelve when we began our preparations to go home. She had already seen more tragedy than most people see in a lifetime. During our escape to Thailand, she witnessed the death of many people during a shelling attack. This particular bombardment occurred during a thunderstorm—a frightening enough experience for a child—so storms became almost unbearable for her. During the bursts of thunder, she would call out, often from beneath her bed, "Daddy! How many more will die today?"

It didn't get any easier for Shalom. One afternoon, during a storm, she was thrown into the air when lightning struck the ground in our section of the camp. Others were flung off their bicycles. Eight people died that day.

I understood her fears, maybe more than I wanted to admit. But one thing I understood even more plainly: Shalom could not find complete security in me, her earthly father. I began to teach her to call out to her Daddy in heaven. Over time, although her fears did not evaporate overnight, she began to learn to pray in earnest. And in learning to pray, she learned to trust God for her own safety.

As security loosened in Site II, I had opportunities to visit other camps. Shalom, ever conscious that she was apt to panic, called out to her heavenly Daddy to protect her earthly one. By 1992, when I attended the mental health congress in Rome, Shalom had become my mightiest young prayer warrior on the home front. She felt an infectious excitement about my trip. Thanks to Shalom's prayers and enthusiasm, when I boarded the plane for Rome, I felt like a bird leaving a cage. Flight never seemed so free.

Our household was larger than ever. In 1989, our three grandsons, Samnang, Rithychan, and Sokha, showed up on our doorstep. Samnang was the first son of Nin, Boury's only son. Rithychan and Sokha were sons of Mom, Boury's daughter. It is a measure of how unstable life in Cambodia remained until the peace accord in 1991 that their parents felt their boys would be safer with us. We were delighted to have them, and they quickly melded into our family unit and the busy ministry life we shared. All three of them are still in ministry today.

We were ready to go home, but when? And how? As we began to thread together the fabric of a plan, the rest of Site II seemed to be unraveling around us. The lawlessness we'd encountered the first few years reemerged. Many of our neighbors fell prey to all kinds of mistreatment. "Guides" would offer to buy their valuables, only to steal them at gunpoint. Others left their homes and their possessions, which became easy pickings for the bands of looters that roamed unhindered in our streets. One evening we heard shots in the Buddhist *wat* down the street. In our culture, the temple is a widely accepted sanctuary.

Things were clearly not good. We looked out our windows and saw a band of men and women carrying watches, shoes, gold, and even heavy sewing machines in a hammock. Our church building and the Hope Christian School just behind it, where we taught English, housed expensive recording equipment. In the church, some frightened people were hiding. We encouraged each other to pray—silently—and watched as the robbers walked right past. That night we realized the tables had indeed turned and our homeland was perhaps a safer environment than Site II. The time for planning was over. It was now time to act.

Shalom clued in right away and asked a million questions: "Do I have brothers and sisters in Cambodia? When will I know I am there? Tell me again what a sugar palm tree looks like? How old is Grandma? Can I take Kiki (her puppy) with me?"

The next day I approached the UN authorities and asked for permission to take the dog with us. Who could deny a 12-year-old girl her puppy?

The Seven-Headed Serpent

Every nation's history holds its own unique horrors. Ours were more recent than most. And every child's personal history has a few moments—a dog bite, a thunderstorm, a ghost story on a dark night—to provide his or her share of fear. Maybe this is why there is frightful imagery in almost every culture's religion. Fear is a universal emotion.

The *nāga* grew out of Hindu mythology and slithered into the Khmer pantheon a few hundred years later. You cannot travel far in Cambodia without encountering the image of one. An imposing *nāga*, a seven-headed serpent, forms a stone balustrade beside a walkway leading into one of the buildings at *Angkor Wat*. Cobralike, it is reared up to strike, revealing its seven human faces. Just a few miles away, the main causeway leading into Angkor Thom is lined by two scaly *nāgas*. An ominous row of *devas* (deities) holds one snake and, opposite them, a row of *asuras* (lesser deities who traditionally compete with the *devas*) grasps another snake. The effect is a grim game of tug-of-war.

The *nāga*, which means "serpent" in Khmer and San-
skrit, is associated with water, either as a protector or as
the instigator of droughts, floods, and other disasters. Although familiar to anyone who has grown up in Cambodia, the *nāga* remains a menacing image. Which is why
it terrified me when I dreamed so vividly of one not long
after we arrived at Site II.

My dream, which I sensed immediately was a vision
from the Lord, began innocently. I saw a pond dotted with
lotus flowers, and beyond it a lovely green pasture. Rows
of lush shade trees lined one side of the field. The trees
were beautiful, but they bore no fruit. Time is hard to
quantify in dreams, but soon I saw a pale horse on the
horizon. As it galloped closer, I knew it was coming to destroy the garden. In my dream I began to speak to the Lord
about what I saw. It was around ten at night, a time when
the entire house was quiet and usually asleep. Boury and
the children overheard me and wondered to whom I
spoke.

I asked the Lord what the dream meant, and it came
to me that the garden was Cambodia. The lotus flower
was an image of Buddha struggling in the mud of sin,
striving to become an enlightened sage. The garden represented a Cambodia that was beautiful but without fruit,
a religion without real hope. The Khmer Rouge had destroyed everything, the infrastructures of our government
and our education and health systems, as well as our free-

dom of religion. We had been a dignified, giving people, but now we were a nation of beggars.

The church would one day gather again, like the bright gems who turned their faces toward the throne. But the presence of the *nāgas* told me the church would be divided.

Next I saw in the field what I took to be gemstones, hundreds and hundreds of different colors and shapes, all dancing in one big sparkling mass. Over and over they sang out, "Hallelujah!" Then I discovered the gems had faces, which they turned to the sky. I looked up and saw a throne. I knew these gems were believers praising God together.

In my dream, I sensed the joy of the moment until I saw it: the *nāga*. There were two of them, one on either side of the throne. I told the Lord, "This can't be Your throne." I experienced the paralysis common to dreamers. Though I wished desperately to warn the praising gems to look out for the Serpent, I could not. I was only an observer.

Then the vision changed, and I saw the tails of both *nāgas* coiled on either side of another throne. Again, I asked the Lord about this throne. Surely it did not belong to Him. Finally, I saw a third throne. This time the *nāgas* were gone and the gemstones were dancing and worshiping freely before God. I knelt then before the throne of grace and joined the others in worshiping Jesus.

The ruts driven into our hearts
by fear were many and deep.
But there was something
more powerful than our fear:
God's love.

When I was fully awake, I pondered these images. They remain with me today, undimmed. I asked the Lord for clarity, and I believe I understood what He wanted me to know. I felt the vision was a warning that the church in Cambodia would one day gather again, like the bright gems who turned their faces toward the throne. But the presence of the *nāgas* told me the church would be divided.

Sadly, this has been the case. The two *nāgas* represented the counterfeit church, and this "church" has been alive and well in Cambodia. In 1989 a group from Canada

called the New Apostolic Church (NAC) entered the
country, and ever since they have caused much division
and deception in the body of Christ.

They claim to be the sole heirs of the apostles. Neither Catholic nor Protestant, the NAC proposes that it
is the only congregation that leads to God, that forgiveness of sins is possible only through them, and that a living
NAC apostle can pray for the salvation of the dead. They
teach that the soul does not go to heaven upon death but
rather to the realm of the departed, where there are various holding areas. The NAC "service for the departed"
supposedly offers a second chance for salvation to the
souls of those who have departed. They defend this "service" by citing Jesus' apparent preaching to the dead mentioned in 1 Peter 3:19–20. The NAC teaches that salvation
is a result of human works, ceremonies, and the works
of Jesus. Their influence brought about a split in the church
in the very early years of our renaissance in Cambodia.

The tails of the *nāga* represented a different kind of
division. Since our return in 1993, the church has been
plagued with two primary problems. First, the varied de-
nominations have not worked together like they did inside
the camps. We would have done well to retain the kind
of collaborative spirit that ruled when we were in exile.
Second, we preserved something we should have jetti-
soned as soon as we were able: a poverty mentality. For
many years the church could not survive without the help

of outside resources; that could not be helped. This dependent spirit has kept us from maturing as we should, and in our immaturity we have suffered further divisions from within. I cannot say I wasn't warned.

I believe this vision, a picture of triumph and worship, but also of danger, intensified my desire to grow the church at Site II into a unified, worshiping, victorious body, so that upon our return, we could take our place as a unified, worshiping, victorious presence in our homeland.

I had good reason to hope. According to the Bible the Serpent—or Satan—is not at all an ambiguous figure. And from the very beginning, he is doomed. Like the *nāga*, he may rear up to strike, but he will not win.

I wasn't the only one who dreamed about a serpent. The apostle John saw the battle between heaven and hell. His words give me a more certain vision of the Serpent's end:

> And the dragon and his angels fought back, but he was defeated, and there was no longer any place for them in heaven. And the great dragon was thrown down, that ancient serpent, who is called the devil and Satan, the deceiver of the whole world—he was thrown down to the earth, and his angels were thrown down with him. And I heard a loud voice in heaven, saying, "Now the salvation and the power and the kingdom of our God and the authority of

his Christ have come, for the accuser of our brothers has been thrown down, who accuses them day and night before our God. And they have conquered him by the blood of the Lamb and by the word of their testimony, for they loved not their lives even unto death." (Revelation 12:7–11)

We would return to Cambodia as we had arrived here: conquering "by the blood of the Lamb and by the word of [our] testimony, for [we] loved not [our] lives even unto death."

Home

As we made our plans based on the limited options available, we fought against a potent and familiar enemy: fear. Just as witnessing a plane crash imbedded fear into my young mind about air travel, fear glides in and creates a channel for even more fear. The uncanny coincidence Shalom experienced with a shelling attack and a thunderstorm, like the fabled *nāga*, wormed into her psyche and turned something God-given—rainfall—into a thing to fear. The ruts driven into our hearts by fear were many and deep. How on earth could we plan for our future when the memories of our past were enough to paralyze us with dread? Yes, our fears were understandable and real. But there was something more powerful than our fear: God's love. "And I am convinced that nothing can ever separate us from God's love. Neither death nor life, neither angels nor demons, neither our fears for today nor our worries about tomorrow—not even the powers of hell can separate us from God's love" (Romans 8:38 NLT).

The fears of our "today" had given us plenty of reasons to worry about our tomorrow. That's because our yesterday had been horrific by just about any measure. Any measure but God's love.

And so, looking our fears full in the face, we considered the options.

We could travel to Battambang in northwestern Cambodia, and once there accept fifty US dollars from the UN in order to buy land. That was enough to buy a parcel of land outside one of the towns. If we took the money, everything else would be up to us.

Or we could be given safe passage to our ancient villages and claim the land that had been ours before the Khmer Rouge took it from us. The only problem with this plan was that there was no guarantee the land would not be occupied by squatters who felt entitled to it. If this were the case, we would then be shuttled to a holding center—now *that* sounded familiar—until the authorities could sort things out.

The misinformation—or complete dearth of information—from home was staggering, and it didn't seem wise to accept this second choice. Either way, we knew the first stop would be Battambang, which was the closest city to Site II.

No one knew how long the peace plan would last— or if it would work at all. But little by little, we began to hear encouraging news. The refugees who left before us had been welcomed. They were settling down and able to write letters, and the letters actually made it to us.

In the end, we decided to go back to Phnom Penh. We also decided we would not accept the UN assistance money. We had a few hundred dollars of our own, but no land, no house, no church. A dry well, indeed. But what we did have—God's love—was an overpowering torrent.

On March 14, 1993, my family and I boarded a bus at Site II. For the first time since becoming a family, we were able to travel together. We made a quick stop at Khao I Dang to pick up our friend Mr. Bunsat and his family. The UN had procured a house for him in Pursat near a school where his children could attend. What a joy to see him. He was still paralyzed, but his heart was pliable and whole. He was not the same man who had tried to end his life years before.

As we rode through the checkpoints and out into the Cambodian countryside, I felt the anxiety of the previous decade melt away. I knew the emotional impact of the past years could not—even should not—be erased so easily. But for the moment, a wonderful moment, the little pleasures of home were more than enough. These small familiarities—workers in wide-brimmed hats out in the fields, motorbikes zipping along with up to three people on the narrow seat and a stream of ocher dust behind, pale oxen pulling wooden carts—these would have seemed insignificant to me before the Killing Fields. But now each reminder of a happier past was fraught with unbridled bliss.

I leaned back and took in the wide, cloudless sky. I could hardly stay in my seat. St. Augustine speaks of becoming "an Alleluia from head to toe," and that is how I felt. I pointed out the traditional Khmer homes along the way, bamboo houses on stilts with steeply pitched roofs. I nodded toward the serene, glassy spans of water that were speckled with greening spears shooting toward the blue Khmer sky. Those, I told the children, are rice paddies. The scene beyond the window of our bus flew past and began to look more and more like home. I scanned the roadside, and finally I saw what I had been looking for. I smiled at Boury and then alerted the boys and Shalom. "There's a sugar palm tree!" I told them.

"Now we are home," Shalom said.

"Yes," I said. "Yes, we are."

EPILOGUE

Your beauty and love chase after me
every day of my life. I'm back home in
the house of God for the rest of my life.

—Psalm 23:6 THE MESSAGE

WE WERE back home. But what does home really mean? If it means—as the Scriptures assert—a secure place to abide in the presence of God, then I had been home all along. Dr. Stanley Mooneyham said, on that night in 1972 when I first ran into the arms of my Father, "To become a Christian is not to accept a Western religion, it is to come home." That very night, I was home.

When I fled Phnom Penh in 1975, I was home. Shackled to a bamboo cot in Sambok Moan, I was home. I was even home in the Killing Fields near Battambang. All along the way to Site II, I was home. And the beauties of home described in Psalm 23—rest, protection, peace, goodness, and mercy, to name only a few—were at my disposal as much then as now.

The love of God had chased me from Phnom Penh to Thailand and back again. The words of Psalm 23 were never far behind:

> The Lord is my shepherd; I have all that I need. He lets me rest in green meadows; he leads me beside peaceful streams. He renews my strength. He guides me along right paths, bringing honor to his name. Even when I walk through the darkest valley, I will not be afraid, for you are close beside me. Your rod and your staff protect and comfort me. You prepare a feast for me in the presence of my enemies. You honor me by anointing my head with oil. My cup overflows with blessings. Surely your goodness and unfailing love will

pursue me all the days of my life, and I will live in the house of the Lord forever. (NLT)

In these past few years, I've had time to read Psalm 23 with more attention and a bit less desperation. Its words are still true of Jesus, my Good Shepherd, and of me, His lamb. My cup does indeed overflow. In Cambodia our cup overflows with blessings.

At the risk of seeming glib about our "darkest valley," I can't help but report that God has brought the miracle of new life to Cambodia. In 1972, the year of my conversion, a wave of spiritual awakening washed over us. In just five years, the church had grown from seven hundred believers to ten thousand. And then in 1979, it is estimated there were only two hundred of us left.

"You are so blessed to follow Jesus. We want to know Him, too. When are you going to tell us about Him?"

Soon after we arrived in Phnom Penh in 1993—for the first time in twenty years—pastors from all over the nation met together in one place. This gathering, at the

Russian Cultural Center in Phnom Penh, was a time of teaching and refreshing. But it was much more than that. Together, four hundred of us prayed for a revival in Cambodia that would surpass the outpouring of God's Spirit we had seen in the early 1970s.

The Flowing Stream

In 1993 my mother and sister came to faith and were baptized in their villages. In 2005, Pastor Khem Sanith, Pastor Lim Sophal, and I joined my mother in handing out boxes donated by Samaritan's Purse to each child at the Trapaing Chak Primary School near her village. A few months later, we visited again and helped my mother take gifts to the poor and the elderly.

On both occasions the villagers were astonished by my family's outpouring of love to those in need. In their eyes such generosity was scandalous, unheard of. A relative of mine, Vanna, asked, "Uncle, you are so blessed to follow Jesus. We want to know Him too. When are you going to tell us about Him?"

"Today!" I said. "Right after lunch I will share the good news about Jesus at your home."

That afternoon, thirty people invited Jesus Christ to be their Lord and their Savior. Pastor Sanith has continued to disciple these new believers. As he got to know and love them, he discovered that the villagers had to travel a long distance every day to a pool to provide water for their families. Sanith and the church that now meets at Vanna's house wrote a proposal to AFCI Cambodia (Ambassadors for Christ International) about the issue. With the help of Living Water Fellowship and Samaritan's Purse Australia, there is now a deep well and a pump right in front of the house church in Trapaing Chak village.

A Feast Prepared

To summarize on a few pages the nearly two decades since leaving Site II is perhaps as foolish as my childhood attempts to number the stars. But sometimes folly is the mother of joy.

When we left Phnom Penh in 1975, a little more than sixty believers met in three underground churches. When the refugees at Site II dispersed, fifty-three trained church leaders and members of fifteen thriving churches made their way back to Cambodia.

With my friend Paulerk's assistance, Boury and I planted Living Hope in Christ Church in Phnom Penh almost immediately upon our return. This church now has forty satellite churches nationwide.

In 2001, I joined Ambassadors for Christ International. Together we established three schools: the Institute of Church Planting, the School of Discipleship Training, and the School of Pastoral Ministry. In the past ten years, thirty pastors have graduated annually from the Institute of Church Planting, and more than four hundred churches have been established. I now oversee the work of AFCI in all of Asia.

It's as if the starving Cambodian church, a body of believers so bereft of nourishment that we almost died, has had a feast laid out on the table before us. We've added leaves to widen the table and legs to keep it from toppling under the weight of so much bounty. These days we are feasting.

The number four hundred doesn't just represent organizations called churches. People are coming to Christ in droves. It isn't rare to attend a baptism of 300, 500, 700, even 1,000 people. Local pastors perform these baptisms, and I, filled with joy, watch my younger brothers wade into the river or lake with so many new believers. It is a feast for my eyes.

The streams of God's goodness are flowing in Cambodia today. And the result is exactly what the psalmist said. One little phrase, slipped into the beginning of Psalm 23, reminds me of the Shepherd's intended outcome through every twist and turn, every hill and valley, at every table.

He leads, we follow, and it is all "for his name's sake" (NIV). Together, we are "bringing honor to his name" (NLT). In an amazing act of solidarity, the Shepherd and His sheep share the same goal. The glory of God.

I began my story by telling you about worship in a Cambodia that was essentially a prison state. It ends with worship in a healing Cambodia. The common thread is worship of a God who is ever worthy. *This* is what it means to be home.